ed by John Wiley & Sons, Inc., Hoboken, New Jersey
ed simultaneously in Canada

of this publication may be reproduced, stored in a retrieval system, or transmitted in any
by any means, electronic, mechanical, photocopying, recording, scanning, or otherwise,
s permitted under Section 107 or 108 of the 1976 United States Copyright Act, without
e prior written permission of the Publisher, or authorization through payment of the
iate per-copy fee to the Copyright Clearance Center, 222 Rosewood Drive, Danvers, MA
978) 750-8400, fax (978) 646-8600, or on the web at www.copyright.com. Requests to the
r for permission should be addressed to the Permissions Department, John Wiley & Sons,
River Street, Hoboken, NJ 07030, (201) 748-6011, fax (201) 748-6008, or online at www
m/go/permissions.

Liability/Disclaimer of Warranty: While the publisher and author have used their best
preparing this book, they make no representations or warranties with the respect to
racy or completeness of the contents of this book and specifically disclaim any implied
es of merchantability or fitness for a particular purpose. No warranty may be created or
d by sales representatives or written sales materials. The advice and strategies contained
ay not be suitable for your situation. You should consult with a professional where
ate. Neither the publisher nor the author shall be liable for damages arising herefrom.

ral information about our other products and services, please contact our Customer Care
ent within the United States at (800) 762-2974, outside the United States at (317) 572-3993
17) 572-4002.

blishes in a variety of print and electronic formats and by print-on-demand. Some material
with standard print versions of this book may not be included in e-books or in print-on-
If this book refers to media such as a CD or DVD that is not included in the version you
d, you may download this material at http://booksupport.wiley.com. For more information
ley products, visit www.wiley.com.

f Congress Cataloging-in-Publication Data:
ilko, Dave, author.
ional persistence : seven business secrets that turned a crazy
nto a #1 national brand / Dave Zilko.
n: Hoboken, New Jersey : John Wiley & Sons, [2016] | Includes index.
: LCCN 2015043063 (print) | LCCN 2016000691 (ebook) |
81119240082 (hardback) | ISBN 9781119240099 (pdf) |
1119240105 (epub)
LCSH: Zilko, Dave, 1963- | Garden Fresh (Firm) | Snack food
—United States. | Businesspeople—United States—Biography. |
neurship. | Success in business. | BISAC: BUSINESS & ECONOMICS /
neurship.
on: LCC HD9219.U64 G379 2016 (print) | LCC HD9219.U64 (ebook) |
8.7/66458—dc23
available at http://lccn.loc.gov/2015043063

the United States of America

6 5 4 3 2 1

DAVE ZIL

FORMER VICE CHAIRMAN OF GA

IRRATIOI
PERSISTE

SEVEN SECRETS THAT TURNED A BA
INTO A $231,000,000 BU

WILEY

Cover
Cover

This bo

Copyri

Publish
Publish

No par
form or
except
either t
approp
01923, (
Publish
Inc., 11
.wiley.c

Limit of
efforts i
the accu
warrant
extende
herein n
appropr

For gene
Departn
or fax (3

Wiley pu
included
demand.
purchase
about W

Library
Names: Z
Title: Irra
startup
Descripti
Identifiers
ISBN 97
ISBN 978
Subjects:
industry
Entrepr
Entrepr
Classificat
DDC 33
LC record

Printed i

10 9 8 7

—————

TO MY PARENTS,
DON AND ARLEEN, WHO INSTILLED IN THEIR CHILDREN
THAT ANYTHING IS POSSIBLE IN THIS LIFE AS LONG AS YOU
BELIEVE YOU CAN DO IT. AND TO MY SONS, CHRISTIAN AND ALEX,
IN THE HOPE THAT THIS DEMONSTRATES HOW TRUE THAT IS.

CONTENTS

Contents

"Nothing in this world can take the place of persistence. Talent will not: nothing is more common than unsuccessful men with talent. Genius will not: unrewarded genius is almost a proverb. Education will not: the world is full of educated derelicts. Persistence and determination alone are omnipotent. The slogan 'press on' has solved and always will solve the problems of the human race."

Calvin Coolidge

PROLOGUE

WHAT'S IT LIKE TO TAKE A BANKRUPT startup and eventually sell it to a Fortune 500 company for almost a quarter of a billion dollars?

This is a different type of business book, one that tells a story—an "Only in America" story.

Just not from the place in America you'd expect.

"Salsa from Detroit? You're kidding, right?"

We'd hear it all the time, and frankly I couldn't blame anyone for asking the question. It's counterintuitive at the very least and borders on irrational.

I'd love to say the idea was born out of some ultra-chic marketing incubator. Where some bold and brilliant entrepreneurs concluded launching a fresh salsa company from Detroit was "so crazy it just might work" and "all we'll need now is a slick ad and PR campaign and we'll be on our way."

But to be honest, we're not that clever.

Instead, Garden Fresh Gourmet was born in the back of a small bankrupt restaurant just outside of Detroit when a 44-year-old man named Jack Aronson pulled out a five-gallon bucket and in 15 minutes developed a recipe for fresh salsa.

"I was just hoping to pay my electric bill," Jack has since told me.

When I first met Jack and his wife, Annette, five years after he made that first batch of fresh salsa, they were still struggling, although no longer bankrupt. I, however, technically could not say the same; 11 years earlier I had founded my own food company on a $2,500 credit card loan, and let's just say things were not going too well for me.

Soon after I met the Aronsons they invited me to be their partner and, despite our humble origins, Garden Fresh is now the largest brand of fresh salsa in the United States with-annual revenues well in excess of $100 million.

And Garden Fresh was just sold to the Campbell Soup Company for $231 million.

We all want to live the life we've imagined for ourselves. For most of us doing that does not just happen; we have to make it happen. Doing so requires sacrifice — often tremendous sacrifice. Sacrifice unimagined in common hours.

I refer to those 11 years between the time I founded my company on that $2,500 credit card loan and the time I met the Aronsons as my "lost decade." And Jack and Annette had had a couple of lost decades of their own before we became partners. On top of that, it took us another decade to fully realize the company Garden Fresh would eventually become.

We persisted against seemingly insurmountable odds in a fashion that can only be described as irrational.

Just as salsa from Detroit is irrational.

It's not lost on me, though, that a lot of people work hard, are determined, yet don't make it, don't end up living the life they've imagined for themselves. Very often there's a missing strategic link that is the difference between success and failure.

Failure's in vogue right now, and for good reason; failure is important in a lot of ways; we all learn more from our mistakes than we do from anything else. We should not fear it. Thus, I'm fine accepting it, even embracing it, as a necessary speed bump on the road to success.

But I've done it enough in my life to confidently state: failure's overrated.

Another thing I can confidently state: it's not as necessary as some people might lead you to believe. We can all learn from other people's experiences.

In this book I share our experiences, a heartfelt story that only life itself could write, as well as the secrets that drove Garden Fresh from the back of that tiny restaurant to become the premiere deli supply company in the United States.

So that you can begin to live the life you've imagined for yourself. Ideally a lot quicker than we did.

INTRODUCTION

Starting with Less Than Nothing

JACK AND I WERE WITH A GUEST in our conference room in Garden Fresh's administrative offices. The company had just hit the $100 million mark and the local media had picked up on it. Our guest was amazed and could not contain himself:

"You know what I like about you two? You guys started with nothing, no one ever gave either of you a thing. I really respect that."

Jack was taken aback by the statement, and answered the only way he knew how:

"Started with nothing? That would have been easy. What's hard is starting with less than nothing."

Our guest was perplexed.

"Dave," Jack asked, "how much debt were you in when we got together?"

"Do you want the real number or just what I'll admit to?

"Let's just go with what you'll admit to."

"$350,000 . . . and I'm glad my wife doesn't read what I give her to sign, no sense both of us losing sleep at night."

Jack proceeded to throw a $450,000 figure on the table, but I knew that too was only what he'd admit to—for a while it seemed every other day someone was showing up at our office reminding Jack of the money they had lent him, and we always seemed to be paying them back.

Jack continued with our guest: "When we add it all up, it was easily a million-dollar hole. Starting with nothing would have been a blessing. Starting with less than nothing—now that's a challenge."

So how did we, me with a couple business degrees from a couple well-respected universities, and Jack, who now deserves to be considered one of the premiere food entrepreneurs in America, find ourselves middle-aged and starting with less than nothing, to the tune of about $1 million?

For me it all started when I was in college. I spent the summer between my sophomore and junior years studying in France, where I absolutely fell in love with the culture. I was just enamored by how wonderful their food was, and even more so by how the French use the occasion of the meal to bring people together. Those people have truly mastered everyday life.

The following summer I interned at a General Motors financial office and realized that working in that world wasn't connecting with me, but what was were the marketing classes I was taking at Michigan State. The strategic aspects of marketing fascinated me, and I was compelled to earn an MBA in marketing, which I did from The George Washington University.

My first job in the real world after I graduated, selling financial securities, was underwhelming, to say the least.

I was not only bored but realized I was not living the life I had imagined for myself. There was simply a gap between the level at which I was living my life, in terms of both professional and financial fulfillment, and the level at which I wanted to live my life.

And that void was simply unacceptable to me. It was driving me crazy.

So I decided to do something about it.

I combined my love of food with my passion for business and started a food company.

I then proceeded to do what just about every food entrepreneur does—spent four months at my kitchen counter developing a line of chicken and beef marinades, came up with the name "American

Connoisseur," hired a graphic designer for $15 per hour, and stood over her shoulder while she created some labels.

When she finished she printed one copy of each, laminated them, and I stuck them on four bottles, then sent them to the buyer at what was then Dayton Hudson Marshall Field's, now known as Macy's.

One night the buyer called me at home—I certainly did not have an office—and said, "These are the best marinades I've ever had. I'm going to place an order," which he did, for 96 cases.

That was the good news.

The bad news was I did not have a place to produce them.

Somehow I stumbled across a guy who owned a small industrial park in metro Detroit. He told me he just had a tenant move out who had a kitchen used for breaks. "Why don't you convert that to a commercial kitchen and see what you can do?"

I thought it was a great idea and, after some research, determined that it would cost $2,500 to convert this 300-square-foot space to a licensed food processing facility.

Well, that was $2,500 more than I had at the time, so I did what every red-blooded American entrepreneur does when he wants to launch a business but does not have the money to do so: I applied for a credit card loan with Discover.

Discover, seeing that I did not have a reliable income but seeing that I did have tens of thousands of dollars in student loan debt, turned me down.

So I proceeded to do what every red-blooded American *male* entrepreneur does when he wants to launch a business but does not have the money to do so *and* is turned down for a credit card loan: I reached out to my girlfriend.

She must have seen something in me and decided to sign for it.

So while I'd love to say that I founded my company on a credit card loan, in reality I was so broke I founded it on my girlfriend's credit card loan.

And people ask me all the time: I not only paid her back, but I did marry her. And we're still married to this day.

A mere 11 years later I found myself, now hundreds of thousands of dollars in debt, at a food show in New York where I approached another metro Detroit food entrepreneur, Jack Aronson.

A few years beforehand Jack founded a fresh salsa company, which he called Garden Fresh Gourmet, in the back of his 1,200-square-foot restaurant. I asked him whether he'd be interested in me bottling some of my products under his label.

Jack thought it was a great idea and after we returned home we got together for lunch and he began to share his saga.

Five years before we met, Jack found himself in the previously mentioned $450,000 hole, 44 years old with no formal education and no formal training, running a tiny restaurant called Clubhouse Bar-B-Q, just outside of Detroit. Jack had to declare bankruptcy to hold onto his lease, was taking the bus to work as his car had been repossessed, and was having tax issues with the IRS.

Desperate, one day Jack pulled out a five-gallon bucket, peeled some onions by hand and in 15 minutes made what is today known as Garden Fresh Artichoke Garlic Salsa.

Jack started putting his salsa on the tables of the Clubhouse Bar-B-Q; after a few weeks, people were standing in line on Friday and Saturday nights to get in.

One day, out of nowhere, Jim Hiller, owner of an upscale chain of metro Detroit supermarkets that bears his name, walked in and told Jack one of his employees said he just had to try Jack's salsa. Jim told Jack that he had been looking for a good fresh salsa for 20 years to no avail, and he asked Jack to whip him up a batch.

Jack did. Jim liked it and asked Jack to start making it for his six-store chain.

Thus, what is today the best-selling brand of fresh salsa in America was innocently born.

Soon, in addition to Hiller's Markets, every party store in the area started picking up Jack's salsa. Word starting getting out about how good Jack's salsa was, so a local news station, Fox2 Detroit, decided to do a story on this eccentric guy making this salsa in the back of his restaurant.

There's an old maxim that says there's no such thing as bad publicity. That's generally true, unless your city manager is sitting at home watching Fox2 news, aghast at this guy making salsa in the back of an unlicensed restaurant in his town.

So the next day he showed up and threatened to shut Jack down. Jack, though, befriended him, and together they found a former video store nearby, with floor to ceiling windows, which Jack converted to a salsa factory.

Jack and his wife, Annette, and their five children now found themselves making salsa for 10 to 12 hours per day, and Garden Fresh Gourmet continued to grow. After a few years, it was finally picked up by a major Midwest chain, Meijer.

A local developer then convinced Jack to build a 25,000-square-foot plant, which he did. It opened just when I first met Jack in New York.

Which brings us to our lunch when we got back to Detroit from the conference.

"You know," Jack said, "everyone told me I was crazy to go from 3,000 square feet to 25,000 square feet, that you don't increase your size eightfold, and I'm starting to think they're right. Why don't you move your business in with me, outsource your manufacturing to Garden Fresh. That will help pay my rent, and I'll give you a free office—you can focus on sales and marketing, whatever you want."

I did just that, and after a few months our talents seemed to complement each other, so Jack asked me to be a partner in Garden Fresh.

That first year together, 2002, Garden Fresh recorded $4.6 million in sales. I distinctly remember meeting with Jack and saying, "If we could ever get this to $10 million and pay attention to our margins, wouldn't that be a great life?"

Well, that seemed to happen in about 15 minutes.

By the middle of the decade, we were up to $30 million in sales and recently crossed the $100-million revenue mark. Garden Fresh is now the number 1 brand of fresh salsa in the United States.

We eventually made our way up to become the third-largest hummus manufacturer in this country, the largest brand of tortilla chips merchandised in the deli, developed a top-ten line of dips, ship over a million units a week, and in the midst of all this, received offers from some of the largest food companies in the world.

All before being approached by the Fortune 500 company that would eventually purchase us.

Doing all this wasn't easy. In fact, there were long stretches when there were more bad days than good. We were often stunned, and often heartbroken, over what was happening to us.

But it was an adventure. In fact, the adventure of a lifetime. Through it all we uncovered powerful secrets that directly led to our success.

In *Irrational Persistence* I describe both our adventures and our misadventures.

Adventures that illustrate that you're not alone with respect to the challenges you might face.

Misadventures that will enable you to avoid our mistakes as you face those challenges.

Secrets that can be applied directly to the challenges. Secrets that can help not only the entrepreneur but that are valuable for the multinational company as well.

Secrets you can implement to accelerate growth and minimize risk.

Secrets that illustrate that, while I hope you never find yourself in the position we did, starting with less than nothing, even under those conditions building something great is still possible.

1

Summon the Courage to Enter the Dark Room

"If you're going through hell, keep going."

–Winston Churchill

So how do you launch a business, even with less than nothing, and somehow get to the point at which some of the largest companies in the world want to buy you?

What's the first step?

The first step is into the dark room.

The dark room is what confronts everyone who is not living the life they've imagined for themselves. Who is professionally unfulfilled. Who finds that condition unacceptable.

And who is determined to do something about it.

And also those who determine that doing something about it involves developing a product or service, then launching it, either within an existing company or doing so independently on their own.

It's one thing to have an idea. Actually making it a reality is another entirely. Actually bringing it to life requires facing a moment of truth.

What's that moment like?

Imagine you're standing in front of a door that leads into a room. A dark room, a room completely devoid of light.

Dark rooms are frightening, potentially filled with peril. There is tremendous ambiguity involved.

It's natural, and certainly rational, to walk away from a situation like that. To not enter the dark room. To stay where you are, where you can at least see what's around you. Where you're comfortable.

But it takes courage, which is often irrational, to enter that room. And to have the door close behind you.

You're now alone. In utter blackness. Not sure where to go. Not sure what to do.

No one is comfortable in a situation like that. It's unpleasant at best, and often terrifying.

So what do you do then?

You search for sources of light to illuminate the dark room. Sources of light that will allow you to navigate your way around the room. That will allow you to be successful in the room so that you're not operating in the dark.

Those sources of light are not always obvious. They can, in fact, take years to locate.

Both Jack and I did enter dark rooms, and we both spent years in them, years in which we often found ourselves in absurd situations doing things we never thought we'd do.

What was it like? What were our darkest moments? Why did we stay in them for as long as we did? Why did we persist?

How did we find the lights to illuminate our dark rooms, so that we could see the paths we needed to be successful? To live the lives we had imagined for ourselves?

LIFE IN THE DARK ROOM: DAVE

So my girlfriend just financed my new food company, American Connoisseur, by signing for a $2,500 credit card loan and I set up shop in a 300-square-foot former break room in a vacant office in a small industrial park in tiny Sylvan Lake, Michigan.

You don't get much for that kind of money, even in the early 1990s. Washable walls and ceiling, a couple sinks; fortunately, my landlord had just closed a TCBY yogurt shop he owned, so he let us borrow a stainless steel table. For equipment I ran to K-Mart and purchased two standard household blenders, some one-quart plastic pitchers, and four funnels.

I found a bottle supplier in downtown Detroit, along with a spice importer, and would make the 35-minute trek one way in my car for supplies. I could fit 35 cases of bottles in my trunk and would buy 20-pound bags of dehydrated garlic, onion, oregano, and basil, all of which would go in my back seat. I'd travel back to our plant with my windows open, even in the winter, to try to dilute the pungent odor from the garlic, but nevertheless the smell would permeate the fabric of the seat upholstery and would last for weeks. For just about everything else — salt, sugar, and canola oil — I'd go to Sam's Club.

To make our marinades I'd measure the ingredients into the blenders, mix them, pour them into a plastic pitcher, put a funnel in the bottle, and fill them, then seal them and label them. All by hand.

The blenders invariably broke down every few weeks — I soon learned the hard way that canola oil seeping into the control panel is not a good thing — and I'd run back to K-Mart to buy $30 replacements.

We did have air conditioning but, ironically, we had no heat. I kept calling my landlord, who lived in the Bahamas for half the year for tax purposes, if that tells you anything, and he just kept telling me to keep flicking the switch on the thermostat and the heat would kick in.

Apparently, the $300 per month in rent I was paying him under the table did not justify a significant capital expenditure budget.

We kept flicking that switch, but nothing ever happened. I wasn't, though, going to let something like the lack of heat stop me. I was in business, and that was all that mattered.

I estimate we did the first 400,000 bottles this way, through five Michigan winters. We could see our breath when we first walked in. My parents gave me a couple of space heaters and after a while that, coupled with our body heat, brought the temperature up to a relatively humane level.

No worries in the summer, however, as again we had air conditioning.

For the most part we'd make our product at night, and in the day I'd balance my time between the various commission-only jobs I arranged, either selling commercial real estate or life insurance, while also trying to market my line of premium marinades.

I was actually getting some nice publicity, even being interviewed by the Food Network on their daily "TV Food News and Views" show.

After taping my segment with one of their hosts, *The Dean & Deluca Cookbook* author David Rosengarten, he was kind enough to escort me out of their Manhattan studios down to the street.

Rosengarten was also at the time the New York City restaurant critic for *Gourmet* magazine. I asked him whether he had any idea how much money he spent dining in Manhattan per year.

"Funny you should ask that," he replied. "They have me use a dedicated American Express Gold Card for all my restaurant meals for the magazine. Just last week I was looking at my statement, and so far this year I've charged just under $95,000 to the card."

This was in early November. Nice work if you can find it.

And sure enough I was getting picked up by local food retailers and then by a few national accounts as well. T.J. Maxx, for example, who had just started selling specialty food, and even QVC, who featured my marinades for years.

Although accounts were buying my products, getting it to them was another story.

Heat wasn't the only thing I was lacking in my little makeshift 300-square-foot kitchen. I couldn't afford a forklift either.

Every time I needed to ship an order, I'd wheel all our product out on a cart into the parking lot, load it onto a pallet on the truck by hand, stretch wrap it myself, and use the truck's pallet jack to get it into the back of the trailer.

After a while it was difficult to even get trucks to come, as sometimes they'd be there for upwards of an hour.

One day a woman, Michelle Marshall, came out into the parking lot. About a decade before, she had started a specialty food company of her own, launching a British pub style mustard she called Mucky Duck, and by chance her kitchen was directly across from mine.

I'd like to think Michelle felt sorry for me, seeing me loading pallets in the snow. In reality she had a doctor's appointment and could not get out of the parking lot, as the truck was blocking her way. She blessedly offered to let me use Mucky Duck's forklift.

That soon became a standard practice for us, and I befriended her as well; I thought she was terrific personally and professionally and believed she had developed a great product, verified by the fact that Mucky Duck Mustard won the 1996 World Championships of Mustard.

A few years after that chance first meeting, after I had been encouraging Michelle to partner with me, she said she was retiring and moving to Phoenix and that if I wanted to buy Mucky Duck, now was my chance.

We closed on the company three weeks later, an all-cash deal that the bank financed 100 percent, with my dad guaranteeing the $108,000 loan.

I figured at least I was consistent: I founded my first company via financing courtesy of my girlfriend and I financed my first acquisition via my dad's credit worthiness.

So now I owned a mustard company, which was very exciting. Even more exciting was that I finally had a somewhat professional commercial kitchen to work out of, and at that time I defined "professional" as having a place with heat and a working forklift.

The day after we closed on the Mucky Duck Mustard Company, we moved across the parking lot to our new professional commercial kitchen. After moving a vertical spice rack we had against the wall in our old American Connoisseur space, one of my employees looked at me, somewhat aghast, and called me over to that wall.

"Uh, Dave—you want to take a look at this?"

I walked over, somewhat concerned, and could not believe what I saw; it was a second thermostat. I flicked the switch, just as my landlord had implored me to do so many times, and sure enough the heat came on. Just as we were leaving the space for the very last time.

An even bigger surprise was waiting for me when I showed up for the first day of production as the new owner of the Mucky Duck Mustard Company.

Most American mustards are made with mustard flour and vinegar that is mixed with maybe turmeric and, when whipped together, comes out as mustard.

It was just my luck, though, that I did not buy an *American* mustard company but one that produced a *British* pub style mustard, which typically have more personality than their U.S. cousins; they're made with eggs and sugar and employ a multi-day process to produce.

So I soon found myself getting up at 5:30 every morning to go in and break eggs for that day's production, something I did for years, and one day I looked back and estimated that the hands that are typing these words now have conservatively broken 800,000 eggs in their lifetime.

Things they don't teach you in grad school...

But I wasn't the only one in our family breaking eggs. My then-girl-friend-now wife Jill, whose signature on that $2,500 Discover credit card loan launched our company, was pregnant with our first child, our son Christian. On her days off from her job working at the cosmetic counter at Neiman Marcus, she would join us in our kitchen and break eggs as well.

As Jill's due date drew closer we found ourselves in our OB-GYN's office and he informed us that Christian was breached and that as a result he'd have to be delivered by Caesarian section. We were thus able to pick a date and time in which Christian would be born.

We subsequently picked a Monday, which the doctor thought was great; then he suggested a time: 11:00 a.m.

I asked if we could make it later that day, as I had a truck coming that morning that I'd have to load. Thus, we scheduled the appointment for 1:00 p.m., and our eldest son was brought into this world about 45 minutes after 1:00 p.m.

The mustard order went out as well that day.

At this point I was six years into my entrepreneurial adventure, still not making money, certainly not enough to raise a family and live on, still piling up debt. Jack and I did not even know each other yet; in fact, we would not even meet for another five years, but it was at this time that his entrepreneurial adventure was beginning, and he was enduring similar experiences with Garden Fresh.

LIFE IN THE DARK ROOM: JACK AND ANNETTE

Like me and my marinades, Jack too started with blenders in the back of his Clubhouse Bar-B-Q restaurant on a little red Formica table.

"It would take me about 20 minutes to make six pints, which I thought was pretty good," Jack recalls. (Today six pints of Garden Fresh Salsa roll off our assembly lines every nine seconds.)

It wasn't long, though, before he sensed that he had something special on his hands. "People started coming from 20 miles away just for this salsa. We couldn't believe it."

As the crowds grew and as more stores in the surrounding area started carrying Jack's salsa he and his wife Annette eventually walled off part of the Clubhouse Bar-B-Q's dining room and converted that to salsa production. They soon realized, though, that their restaurant did not have the cooler capacity to handle their new production levels.

So they rented an 8-by-20-foot walk-in cooler and located it in the back alley of the Clubhouse Bar-B-Q even though doing so violated the local zoning ordinances. Annette soon found herself running outside into the often muddy alley to get their raw materials, then at the end of the production session running finished product back out to it.

It was at about this time that Fox2 News did a story on Jack. "It didn't even dawn on me that we weren't exactly up to code," Jack recalls. "That didn't happen until the city manager showed up the next day."

Together, though, he and the city manager did find a 3,000-square-foot vacant former video store, with the notion that Jack and Annette would convert the space to salsa production.

Before they could, however, they had to petition the city to change the zoning from commercial to industrial.

Jack remembers the city council meeting in which he tried to do just that: "Some of the council members were against the zoning change, saying that the highest and best use for this space was still commercial, not industrial. So I told them I'd set up a card table just inside the front entrance, that I'd call it a 'store,' and promised to sell a pint of salsa to any member of the public who walked in for $2.50." This was good enough for the council, and the zoning change was approved.

Although we were located 15 miles apart and were not to meet each other for another five years, both my American Connoisseur Gourmet Foods/The Mucky Duck Mustard Company and Jack and Annette's Garden Fresh Gourmet were both now operating out of 3,000-square-foot production facilities.

As I was getting up at 5:30 a.m. to go in and break eggs for that day's production, Annette would arrive at the former video store an hour earlier than that to move all the packaging materials from the production floor out to the parking lot, just so they'd have the room to produce Garden Fresh Salsa.

When it rained or snowed, which happens often in Detroit, Annette would run out to the lot and cover everything with tarps.

This was after she'd label the salsa cups the previous evening, at home, by hand. She says, "I'd do about three cases of empty containers, and that would get us through the next day's production."

That would be enough for about 1,500 pints of salsa, or 60 batches worth, which would take Jack, Annette, and their crew of seven upwards of 10 hours, a task that today takes Garden Fresh less than 10 minutes.

Even with all the packaging materials outside, there was still not sufficient room in the old video store for refrigeration, so Jack came up with an ingenious idea.

He'd have his tomatoes dropped off in a refrigerated trailer and move all the tomatoes to one side. They'd then draw down on the tomato inventory throughout the day and store the finished salsa product on the other side of the trailer.

Back inside the plant, Annette would be personally "lidding" every pint by hand. "They all had to be perfect," she says.

When that day's production run was completed, Annette would break out a 12-pack of Corona beer for herself and their employees to enjoy as they cleaned the plant. Finally, they'd move all their extra packing materials back in from the parking lot to the shop floor and call it a day.

But Jack's day was far from over.

He would deliver the fresh salsa himself, often at night, as that was the only time some of the large accounts he had started to land would receive deliveries.

The deliveries did not always go smoothly. . .

One morning, after a particularly long production session the previous day and after delivering product all night, Jack was driving home. After being up for close to 24 hours, he could no longer keep his eyes open, so at red lights he'd put the car in park, close his eyes, and wait for the driver behind him to honk his or her horn when the light turned green, waking Jack up to continue his march home.

After a few years, Garden Fresh was picked up by a major Midwestern chain, Meijer, and Jack was delivering salsa to one of their distribution centers when his truck hit a deer, doing $10,000 of damage to Garden Fresh's only delivery vehicle.

When the tow truck arrived, the driver told Jack he knew of a shop nearby that was open and could repair the truck in maybe a day or so. Jack would hear nothing of it.

"You've got to take me to the Meijer distribution center first," he told the driver. "I can't be late on this order."

The driver was incredulous, but Jack insisted and paid him an extra $300. Meijer did receive the order via Jack's truck that was ushered into the distribution center via a tow truck. The guys at the receiving dock were as incredulous as the tow truck driver; they had never seen anything like this.

Shortly after, Jack received a call from the deli buyer at the largest chain in Florida, Publix, an account he had been trying to land for months.

"You've been calling me forever," the buyer said to Jack. "Someone just cancelled for tomorrow afternoon, so if you want to jump on a plane and get here at 3:30, the appointment's yours."

Jack told him he'd be there. What he did not tell him, though, was that he could not afford a plane ticket, and, even if he did fly, Jack did not trust UPS to get his product there in good condition for the meeting. He subsequently packed his car with fresh salsa samples and drove straight through the night, making the 27-hour trek to Publix' headquarters in Lakeland, Florida.

When Jack pulled up to the security gate the guard, "a dead ringer for the Maytag repairman," Jack recalls, came out and asked whom he was there to meet. Jack was so tired he could not remember the name of the Publix deli buyer, Raul Garcia, so he said the first thing that came to his mind, which unfortunately was not the buyer's name but the name of the Columbian Coffee mascot.

"Juan Valdez," Jack told the guard.

"Never heard of that guy," the guard responded, and subsequently told him to get out of the car and ordered security to check it as Jack frantically called Annette to see who he was supposed to meet with.

After Jack got the name right, the guard said, "We got that guy" and let Jack proceed into corporate headquarters.

So Jack had his meeting with the Publix deli buyer, but did not get the account. That would not happen until years later, after we had become partners.

Today, however, Garden Fresh is the number 1 brand of fresh salsa at Publix, and we also produce their private label salsa as well. They're one of our top ten customers.

A few months after that, on the eve of Jack and Annette's wedding anniversary, Jack had made arrangements to make a delivery to an upscale account in Grand Rapids, about two and a half hours from Garden Fresh's plant.

Jack felt bad about missing their anniversary, so he invited Annette to come with him and reserved a special honeymoon suite at one of the premiere hotels in Grand Rapids.

About halfway between Detroit and Grand Rapids, though, the beleaguered Garden Fresh truck blew a rod, and it was all Jack could do to even move it to the side of the road. Worse yet, Jack could not leave the refrigeration unit running all night so all the salsa for the next day's delivery was at risk.

So he walked up the highway exit ramp into a nearby supermarket and loaded a shopping cart with 50 bags of ice. He then walked back out to the highway, with the shopping cart full of ice, and proceeded to pack the salsa in the ice to keep it cold through the night.

It was then that Jack realized he had spent nearly all his cash on the ice. Luckily, Annette had a $20 bill and the two of them scurried across the highway and spent the evening in a $29 motel room.

"Let's just say it was at that moment I realized the honeymoon was over," Jack recalls. And by "honeymoon" Jack was not referring to his marriage to Annette. He was referring to the thrill of getting a business off the ground.

It was a feeling I was very, very familiar with.

I can smile now about how we made our first 400,000 bottles of marinade by hand with $30 store-bought blenders in a 300-square-foot kitchen with no heat. I do so fondly because, as dire as our circumstances might have appeared to me, it was the most "romantic" time of my business career.

The thrill of having developed a product that someone actually wanted to buy was palpable. Then receiving positive feedback in addition was just an incredible adrenaline rush. That was all I needed to survive.

Resources and profit, or the lack thereof, didn't matter; that would all come later, I believed. For now just the joy of pursuing a dream, of taking the first steps toward living the life I had imagined for myself, that was enough to live on, enough to live for.

As the years go by, though, you begin to realize that maybe delayed gratification, manifesting itself in the form of increasing debt and physical hardship, is not all it's cracked up to be.

In other words the honeymoon does end.

———

IRRATIONAL PERSISTENCE

What Jack and I both learned was that, as much courage as it takes to even enter the dark room, sometimes it takes even more courage to stay in it, as sometimes the room gets even darker before you begin to see the light.

My darkest moment is not something I can smile about. Still.

I had developed that line of salad dressings made with whole cloves of garlic. I was genuinely proud of them. I thought then and still do today that they're the best of their class on the market, and one region of Costco had agreed to test them.

It was a huge order for us, 12 full pallets, and we finished producing it in the morning. My crew then departed, and I worked into the late afternoon in my office waiting for the truck to arrive.

It was late winter and the weather was awful, truly as bad as it gets; cold but not cold enough to snow, with an incessant rain. Any UPS driver will tell you that he'll take snow over a cold rain any day, which has a bone-chilling effect, made worse this particular day by a howling wind.

When the truck finally came, I put on my rain gear and started loading the pallets with my forklift. Another thing they don't teach you in grad school is how to operate one of these puppies—talk about things you never thought you'd be doing with your life.

I'd load a pallet onto the truck, then hop on the bed of the truck to move the product to the back with the driver's pallet jack.

The beds of most commercial transport trucks are essentially steel rails with ridges between them, and when they are wet they're slick.

As I was pulling one of the pallets backwards, I slipped and was heading toward the sidewall of the trailer. I could not hold onto the pallet jack and soon found myself falling, back first, uncontrollably, into the side wall.

Anyone who has ever been in an auto accident knows of the sensation that while you're in the midst of it seems to last indefinitely, even though in reality it is over in an instant. Time seems suspended.

That's what I was experiencing at that moment. The time it took between my hands leaving the pallet jack and the time I hit the wall seemed like an eternity. I remember realizing that I had completely lost control of my circumstances, that this was truly going to be painful, and furthermore I might be seriously injured. I thought for sure I was going to break my back.

Hitting the wall was like a scene out of cartoon, where the character splats up against a barrier and slides down into a heap—that's exactly what transpired.

My first reaction was one of surprise, and some relief, that I was not hurt, but then I just looked around at my surroundings. I was in the back of this unlit truck in this tiny industrial park in suburban Detroit. I was freezing cold, wet, and on the bed of this truck sitting in a pool of water grateful that I thought I could get up.

I cried that night as I was driving home, wondering what the hell I was doing with my life and how it could ever get to this point.

I was in my mid-thirties, with a wife and a young son. Well-educated but still paying off my student loans. Hundreds of thousands of dollars in debt with a company that had never made money, was still not profitable, and frankly had no chance of being so anytime soon. I was selling life insurance at night to make ends meet, all the while spending my days breaking eggs in the morning and putting whole cloves of garlic in salad dressing bottles in the afternoon and operating a forklift in the most miserable weather imaginable.

I just didn't see a way out for myself. On top of that, I had recently had a discussion with a friend of mine who told me he was thinking about retiring soon because his stock options in the tech company he was working for were doing so well.

And yet, I never even considered stopping. Stopping would have been the rational thing to do, but to me, at that time, it would have meant giving up on a dream, and I still believed dreams could come true. Even if they took a long, long time.

And I was used to waiting a long, long time for my dreams to come true.

During that summer I spent in France, I traveled to Paris almost every weekend and was fascinated by what I saw, and by what I felt. It simply possessed a beauty and an elegance that I did not think was possible, and coupling that with the populace speaking a different language made me feel like I was in another world. I loved it... everything about it.

There was one spot in particular that I found particularly poignant; it was a small concrete bench on the banks of the Seine, just across from Notre Dame Cathedral. I was just 20 years old at the time, but I promised myself if I ever decided to share my life with someone I would ask her to do so on this very bench, on the banks of this river in the shadows of this ancient cathedral.

It was at that same age that I met Jill in college, and we started dating shortly thereafter. We stayed together while I was in grad school in Washington and she was working in retail in New York. We both moved back to Detroit after I graduated.

As the years went by, people often wondered, very often aloud, when we'd get married. We were approaching common law, after all, as we had been living together for so long.

I knew exactly why we were not getting married, though. It was because my company was not profitable enough for me to afford a trip to Paris to propose to her on that park bench on the banks of the Seine. I just had to get engaged in that fashion, no matter how long it took. Anything less would be a compromise.

When we were 31, however, again a mere 11 years after we had met, Northwest Airlines (since bought by Delta) ran a deal for a round-trip ticket to Paris for $299. Fortunately, I still had enough room on my credit card for a purchase of that size.

I bought the tickets, but then realized that Jill did not have a passport. Wanting the trip to be a surprise, I had to be creative.

One morning I told her we needed to get our pictures taken for personalized credit cards (back then companies were at times putting your picture on your cards). I used that head shot of her to fill out a passport form, forged her signature, and sent it all to the passport office, paid for expedited processing, and after about a week we were legally able to travel to Paris.

The day before we were scheduled to leave, I surprised her with the trip, telling her I was attending a food show in Paris and that I had made arrangements with her boss at Neiman Marcus for her to be able to come with me.

The following day, after we had landed and checked into our hotel room, I walked her to that very same simple bench on the banks of the Seine and asked her to marry me. It was then she realized there was no food show, that we were in Paris for this reason and for this reason only.

She also realized there was no ring. I could barely afford the money for the expedited passport service, and I certainly did not have enough money for anything else.

My biggest surprise of that moment, though, was realizing the sensation of a dream coming true. I had wanted to propose to someone in this manner for 11 years and now it was happening. I remember thinking: this was worth the wait.

So for me, persisting with my business, despite how irrational it all might have seemed to an outsider at the time, was the only option my heart would allow.

I just could not fathom not living the life I had imagined for myself.

And no matter how long that took, I believed it also would be worth the wait.

Jack tells me he never considered stopping either, and his circumstances were more dire than mine, by virtually every measure: older, more debt, bigger family to support. When I asked him why he kept going, he replied in the simplest manner possible: "We did what we had to do."

———

ILLUMINATING THE DARK ROOM

So I just kept going, believing that I'd figure it out, that somehow, some way, someday I'd find the source, or sources, of light that would illuminate that dark room.

So that I could finally see what I was doing. So that I could find the path that would allow me to navigate my way out of the mess I found myself in.

Prior to going to that food show in New York, where I would introduce myself to Jack, I was in discussions to merge with another food company. I was exploring buying yet another, believing combining my distribution network with theirs would be the answer I was looking for—not that I had any money to buy another company, but that had never stopped me before.

Jack was also looking for sources of light, which would allow him to stop operating in the dark, operating blindly. Which would illuminate a path to success for him and his family.

Which is why he was at that food show in New York, too. He had just opened his new plant, had feared he had overbuilt, and needed to grow, and grow quickly, to make it all work.

When you're looking for sources of light to illuminate the dark room, you'll find that they come with varying degrees of intensity.

When you're in a dark room, any light, even something as small and innocent as a night light, will help.

Introducing myself to Jack, and the two of us subsequently becoming partners, were floodlights. The dark rooms we had entered into so long ago, 11 years for me, almost twice that amount of time for Jack, were finally illuminated.

I, after a lost decade, had finally found a company I could build, and partners with whom to do it.

Jack finally had a platform on which he could operate a real food plant profitably and a partner with whom he could rapidly grow Garden Fresh Gourmet.

What we soon learned, though, was that, if you want to grow your company, you never completely leave the dark room.

You're almost always living with ambiguity. You're constantly accepting more and more risk.

If you are intent on growing, it will require approaching yet another door, a door that leads to an even bigger room that is just as dark as the one you just left.

If you want to grow, you'll have to enter that room, too, then begin the process of searching for additional sources of light so that you can navigate your way around that room also.

And those dark rooms keep coming and coming.

They certainly did for Jack and Annette and me, once we became partners. And they certainly don't get easier to enter as you grow, but at least we weren't in our respective dark rooms alone any more. We were now in there together.

Secret 1: Your Dark Room

Dark rooms exist in all of our professional lives, whether you consider yourself an entrepreneur or not.

What if you're NOT an entrepreneur at heart? I believe that in everyone there is a small but important part that is. There are times in your life when you have taken risks and things have either worked out, or they haven't, but you knew taking the risk was the right thing to do.

Being an entrepreneur does not necessarily mean starting your own company. There are entrepreneurs operating within existing companies, both large and small. Doing incredible things. Creating significant value for themselves, their colleagues, and their owners.

So wherever you might find yourself right now, there are probably opportunities in your life that represent a "dark room" for you.

Where you assess there is a void between the level at which you're living your life and the level at which you want to live your life.

Continued

Continued

Doing something about alleviating that void may involve a large or small amount of risk.

Taking on that risk, taking action despite an uncertain outcome, is challenging.

There's a certain mindset required to take that first step into that dark room, one that demands you accept ambiguity, that insists you be comfortable with being uncomfortable.

Acquiring that mindset doesn't come naturally to everyone.

So often we need both perspective and guidance.

Perspective in the spirit of Martin Luther King's words: "You don't have to see the whole staircase. Just take the first step.

And guidance once you do that.

I've been there—in the dark room where I was operating blindly. Where I could not see where I was going.

Looking back, my biggest surprises are how hard it was to be there and how long it took me to get out of it.

It's not always necessary, though, to spend as much time in the dark room as I did. A lost decade. Or as much time as Jack and Annette did. Multiple lost decades.

Use the secrets we learned the hard way, through experience, so that you can learn them an easier way, through ours.

But you've got to take that first step. If you do, amazing things are possible.

2

Find Your Place in This World

"I remember very clearly Steve announcing that our goal is not just to make money but to make great products."
—Jonathan Ive, Steve Jobs biography by Walter Issacson, page 340

One of the first dark rooms that Jack, Annette, and I found ourselves in revolved around our very essence as a company.

It's a question that any product, service, or enterprise faces.

What promise are you making to your customers? And how will you ensure that that promise is kept throughout every aspect of your customers' experience with your product, with your service, with your company? And how can you ensure that that promise will be maintained over time?

We had to find our place in this world. Where did we fit in?

Doing so meant we had to develop a standard for our brand in general, and for our products in particular.

But in so many ways we were lost, reeling in one dark room after another. We were unsure of ourselves, questioning everything from what we should call ourselves, to what approach we should take to our labels, even to where we were from.

On top of all that, we were faced with almost constant challenges in maintaining the quality of our products. In terms of distributing them outside of our Midwest base as well as whether to compromise our flavor profile in order to maintain our profit margins.

We were searching for our North Star, a light that would illuminate our dark rooms. The standard that would guide us through all the decisions that lay before us.

It was Annette, unknowingly but instinctively, who ultimately provided it for us.

I typically ran our Garden Fresh board meetings, and at one of them we were discussing the Fortune 500 food companies that were starting to enter our deli space. Our lives were getting much more difficult, and there was concern among our board members as to how we'd compete.

Annette was undaunted.

"I don't care who we're going up against. We make great products," she exclaimed.

I was so struck by her strength, by her irrational defiance. The rational thing to do would be to cower in the face of such fierce competition. But to Annette it didn't matter. All that mattered to her was that our products were great.

I was genuinely moved by the spirit of the moment.

"Annette's right," I agreed. "In fact, our products are not only great, but they are the best on the market. And we've just got to believe as long as we're the best there is going to be a place for us in this world."

We adopted that mantra, *as long as we're the best, there is going to be a place for us in this world*, as our brand standard.

It served as our guide, what we reverted to whenever we were faced with a critical decision regarding our company, our brand: we were promising to be the best.

Once you commit to your place in this world, though, you can't compromise from there.

At Garden Fresh, there was one promise we simply had to keep: to be the best products on the market.

We could never have imagined, though, just how difficult it would be to live up to that standard.

––––––

EMBRACE WHAT MAKES YOU SPECIAL

Jack and I were in Los Angeles, meeting with Paul Neumann, the Los Angeles regional deli buyer for Costco.

Costco had become one of the top five retailers in the United States. They are also one of the largest sellers of food as well, moving from their origins as a bulk supplier to restaurants to a surprisingly sophisticated purveyor of everything from meat to seafood to wine that the public was clamoring for every bit as much as restaurateurs were.

They had done so by employing a business model that absolutely stressed quality, strategic partnerships with their supply base, and industry low margins. And by limiting their product selection, often carrying just one or two items per category.

The average supermarket typically offers upward of 60,000 items. Costco limits their count to only 4,000 in their entire building. And only about two-thirds of those are food.

Thus, if you happened to be one of those one or two items in your category, the volume potential was enormous.

Garden Fresh Salsa was not one of Costco's one or two fresh salsas, but I desperately wanted us to be.

For many small companies it takes considerable courage to even approach Costco; it's not easy to figure out and then adapt to their unique club format business model.

Selling to Costco in and of itself is akin to entering a dark room.

But there's one thing about Jack, and I believe this is an essential trait of every successful entrepreneur; his heart irrationally says "yes" before he ever lets his head rationalize him into saying "no." Or even "wait, let's think about this."

It is certainly something he and I have in common.

Thus, when I told him we should try to get into Costco, even though we really had no idea what we were doing, he instinctively said, "Sure, let's do it."

So we were entering into another dark room. Can we really make it at Costco? One of the premier retailers in the United States?

Most national retail chains have one centralized buying entity, one place, often with a single buyer, where product decisions are made for their entire chain.

Not Costco. In order to give their clubs local personality, Costco divides the United States and Canada into ten regional buying offices. Each has to be approached independently, as they all make their own purchasing decisions.

Thus, Jack and I found ourselves in L.A., about as far away from home as we could get and still be in the United States.

Early in our meeting Paul Neumann picked up a pint of Garden Fresh "Jack's Special" Medium Salsa. He studied the label, specifically the side panel where we have our company's contact information listed.

"You two are from Detroit? What'd you do, get lost coming out of Texas? I get 100 fresh salsa companies a year coming through here, and they're all from either Texas or Southern California. You guys are supposed to be making cars in Michigan. Whoever heard of a fresh salsa company coming from Detroit?"

Paul Neumann was not the only one who felt that way. We'd hear it all the time: "Fresh Salsa from Detroit? No way." We heard it so much that for years Jack contemplated getting a post office box in New Mexico and putting that on our label, just to make ourselves look credible.

"I know you want to grow the company outside of the Midwest, Dave," he'd tell me. "And trust me, I do, too. But no one's going to take a salsa company from Detroit seriously. No one wants salsa from Michigan. If we put a P.O. box number from New Mexico on our labels, and just have our checks sent there, we'll look like a salsa company should."

It wasn't just our address that concerned Jack.

Nearly all our main competitors, who were ten times our size in terms of revenue, had names that emanated from the Southwest in some fashion as well. So we wondered whether the name Garden Fresh was really the way to go outside of our home base.

I once asked Jack how he came up with the name "Garden Fresh."

"I really didn't put much thought into it," he told me. "I remember being in the back of my old restaurant and it came to me. It just sounded right."

You can't get more innocent than that, and it was certainly working for us back home. But could "Garden Fresh" truly work as a national brand? Or would we have to come up with something that was indigenous to where people believed salsa originates?

We even bought a tiny salsa company called Gourmet Jose, partly because we thought we might need a Tex-Mex sounding brand.

We found our answers during our journey to live up to our brand promise, to ensure that our products are truly the best, while addressing our label creative.

There are so many aspects involved with being a truly great product, with being the best in your category. In our world, food products, they involve not only how your products taste by how they look.

People buy food with their eyes, at least initially—they certainly cannot taste the product before they take it home. Thus, at the very least a food product's label needs to be attractive, and ideally appetizing.

But even more importantly the products need to attract a consumer's attention.

That's easier said than done. The number of products offered in supermarkets represents an overwhelming, inhuman selection. The average consumer, when pushing a cart down an aisle in a grocery store, spends 1/11th of a second eyeing a product, and in that time must decide whether to study it further. That's about the same amount of time a major league baseball player has to decide whether or not to swing at an incoming pitch.

Not a lot of time. A split second.

So the best labels not only tell the consumer what the product is, fresh salsa, in our case, but also must compel the consumer to pick it off the shelf and then entice him or her to put it in the basket.

Products do that by conveying a certain personality, by indicating what makes the product special, and do so in an artistic fashion, combining both words and graphics.

Garden Fresh's packaging at the time was falling well short of that. What was inside the package was special; what was outside, on its labels, was pedestrian.

I told Jack we needed to do something about that.

One of the first things I did after joining Garden Fresh, after bringing in my accountant, was to reach out to the advertising agency I was employing for my Mucky Duck Mustard Company line. By this time I had moved on from that $15 per hour graphic artist who crafted my old American Connoisseur labels to a professional design group based in suburban Detroit.

Jack agreed to consider improving our labels, and soon we met with my design agency, the Eidos Group.

Jack is 6 feet 5 inches tall, is a chiseled 265 pounds, and to this day is a world champion softball player. (We supply the Detroit Tigers with chips and salsa at their stadium, Comerica Park. For his sixtieth birthday I arranged for Jack to have 15 minutes at home plate, and he proceeded to hit 19 slow pitch softballs over the left field fence, which, by the way, happens to be one of the deepest outfields in the major leagues.) At any given time, he would rather be on a baseball diamond than sitting in a long meeting with a bunch of advertising executives.

But fidget as he almost constantly did, when he wasn't yawning, Jack made it through the nearly two-and-one-half-hour Eidos presentation. Their work was nothing short of brilliant, and at the end they suggested Garden Fresh retain their services for $5,000 per month.

Jack and I got back in the car. I asked him how he felt about what he had just seen. "Well, we certainly don't have an extra $5,000 per month lying around."

I wasn't surprised by that. The raised eyebrows I was receiving from my accountant was an early indicator that Garden Fresh was at the time not exactly cash flow positive. I wasn't taking a salary from Garden Fresh at the time, and would not for another year and a half. I don't think Jack and Annette were taking much out of the company either.

I immediately began to think about what kind of deal I could propose to the Eidos Group to work this out. Deferred payments, perhaps, as I knew we just had to move forward with these guys.

But I did not have to think about it too long, as Jack blurted: "You're right. We need to do this. We'll find the money someplace, somehow. I just hope they don't' expect to get paid on time."

Yet another thing Jack and I had in common: he'd do anything to make his product better, whether we could afford it or not.

So Garden Fresh Gourmet had a professional design agency, and I had the president of The Eidos Group, Mike Griffin, begin to work on upgrading our labels.

But little did we know that it was the desire to make our labels better, so that our product truly was the best on the market, that ultimately convinced us to stay true to who we were. That even though salsa from Michigan was on the surface not necessarily rational and that our brand did not scream where people thought salsa was from that we were still on the right path.

In this instance, Mike provided the light that led us out of this particular dark room. He was the one who helped us secure our place in this world.

The first thing Mike had us do was to decide what we wanted Garden Fresh to stand for, what we wanted it to represent, what the essence of our brand was. In other words, what would we say to the consumer during that 1/11th of a second when he or she took notice to us in the supermarket.

Jack thought that maybe we should focus on the health aspects of our salsa: it's all natural, gluten free, high in lycopines, and has only ten fat-free calories per serving.

Mike, though, suggested we focus on the *use occasion* of our product, or how people actually consumed our salsa.

Then he encouraged us to not just think about how consumers eat our products but how they *experience* our products.

He pointed out that most people eat salsa with tortilla chips, and when they do it's a treat for them. And that very often people share chips and salsa in a communal nature, placing them in the center of a gathering and everyone eats them in a family-style manner, all the while conversing with each other.

"Your product brings people together, in a way that makes them happy," Mike said. "It simply puts a smile on people's faces. Your labels should then put smiles on your customers' faces, too."

The more I thought about what Mike was saying, the more I liked it. So I gave Mike the green light and he eventually distilled our brand personality to the following: A party in a cup.

To say it connected with me is an understatement. I loved it.

Consistent with how Garden Fresh was unlike any other fresh salsa on the market—no Tex-Mex theme; from the Midwest, not the Southwest—Mike proceeded to design a brand standard that was unlike any other salsa on the market. A fun, festive, busy-as-hell label with the widest palette imaginable, what he refers to this day as a "riot of colors."

"Sure, there's a lot going on on these labels," he assured us. "But there's a lot going on at a party, too. People are singing, eating, drinking, dancing, watching TV. Parties are fun, and so is your product."

Fresh vegetables were represented in an animated form and seemed to come alive right before your eyes, almost as if they were dancing. A thermometer, presented in a cartoonish fashion, was off to the right to signify the heat level of the salsa: mild, medium, or hot.

They were major league labels. Genuinely artistic, conveying that we were a serious company producing a serious product. Like our salsa, they put a smile on people's faces.

It was never lost on Mike that this was still salsa and salsa is supposed to be fun. Thus, while these were serious labels, the overall message was that we were secure enough not to take ourselves too seriously.

That's not an easy thing to pull off.

Mike then taught us to believe in the genuine nature of our brand, Garden Fresh Gourmet, and that feigning New Mexican residency was not necessary. He said:

"Every other fresh salsa brand out there names themselves after some fictional Hispanic caricature, or some crazy Southwest Tex-Mex theme, simply because salsa originated from those regions. Garden Fresh, however, is not pretending to be something it's not. In fact, you're more authentic than any of those brands that make up a name believing people will think it's real salsa because it has some cowboy-orientated background.

"If you think about it, who wouldn't want salsa made *fresh* from produce—tomatoes, onions, cilantro—culled directly from their *garden*. In that sense you're more genuine than anything else out there. Isn't that what the Mexicans who created salsa and still make their own do anyway? Don't feel the need to hide behind some made-up Hispanic cartoon figure.

"*Garden Fresh* Gourmet Salsa. That's who you are, but that's what fresh salsa should be: all natural, no preservatives, fresh from your garden, and gourmet. Your product epitomizes that, so does your brand, and now so do your labels.

"And that you're from Detroit just emphasizes even more how different your salsa is. You're not like the other guys. Not being from the Southwest is something to shout about."

Mike had a few other, more esoteric suggestions for us, namely that our labels were too variety-centric as opposed to brand-centric, which he fixed by modernizing the Garden Fresh Gourmet logo and making it significantly more prominent on the front display panel.

I thought the new labels Mike designed were incredible. Jack and Annette, though, needed some time. Garden Fresh was their baby; overall, the product was being well received, and to tinker with it to this extent, to change its packaging, was a decision that did not come naturally.

But in the end we referred to our brand standard, to our place in this world, for guidance. If we were to fulfill our brand promise, to be the best, our labels would have to reflect that commitment.

So we signed off on Mike's new program.

We had always been a best-in-class salsa, but now, with professional labeling to tell the world who we truly were, we were a best-in-class brand as well.

———

BE AUTHENTIC NO MATTER WHAT

Just as we decided not to run from who we were or where we were from, we decided early on to stay true to our product.

At any cost.

Early in our partnership, a guy from Toronto showed up at our plant and asked for me. A few days before, one of the local TV news stations had done a story on us (when you're the largest fresh salsa company in America and you're from Detroit, you tend to be quite the media darlings) and he happened to see it, as you can pick up the Detroit stations in Toronto.

"I saw you guys peeling onions by hand on TV; you don't have to do that," he told me, and proceeded to pull out of his briefcase a bag of perfectly diced, flash frozen onions.

I started eating them out of the palm of my hand, and they were delicious. Being the MBA of the group, with my other hand I pulled out my financial calculator and estimated that we could save $213,000 per year in labor by not buying fresh onions and peeling them by hand.

This was when $213,000 was still a lot of money to us. I told Jack we needed to try this and he agreed.

So we made a sample batch of Garden Fresh salsa and, instead of putting three or four fresh onions in our recipe, we used these perfectly diced, flash frozen onions.

I have a decent palate and could sense the difference; Jack has an amazing palate and could really tell the difference. It turns out fresh onions are comprised of 89 percent water and that water becomes flavored. It's literally onion juice, and if you dice them and freeze them, you lose all that water, all that flavor.

So while at the time $213,000 was all the money in the world to us, we reverted back to our brand standard for guidance. We believed that as long as we were the best there would be a place for us in this world. That was the essence of our brand promise, and this was not the time or the way to compromise on our quality.

To this day Garden Fresh uses fresh onions in all our salsa. And we still peel them by hand, though not for lack of trying to find a better way.

Jack was at an equipment show one year and bought a machine that peeled the onions for us. After trying it for a while, we realized it was bruising the onions, which fostered fermentation, which is not good for fresh salsa.

When fresh vegetables ferment, they produce a gas. In an airtight container that gas has no place to go, so our products would bloat; the plastic expands and looks like a football. The salsa is still safe to eat, but due to the optics the product is unsalable.

So out went the onion peeling machine, soon followed by yet another onion peeling contraption.

A salesman showed up at our plant hawking this air gun that you pointed at an onion and it would blow the peel right off. Jack was excited, as he thought this would not only reduce our labor costs but that it would be a cleaner process as we would not be touching the onions anymore.

Jack, to his credit (everyone in the food industry should be this way), is obsessed with cleanliness—it's hard to go 15 feet in any of our facilities without coming across a hand sanitizing station—to the point we often jokingly refer to him as "Howard Hughes."

In all honesty, we were only half-joking.

So we installed this air gun, and soon after I'm getting calls from our buying offices all over the country, complaining that our salsa is bloating. Fermentation is occurring due to bacteria still living in our fresh vegetables.

I asked Jack if he changed anything in our production process. He swore he didn't, telling me: "The only thing we're doing differently is using the air gun to peel the onions, but that's got to be cleaner, as we're no longer touching the onions with our hands."

The bloating persisted so Jack finally hired a processing consultant to come in and review our procedures, and after a while decided to check the hose on the air gun.

Thanks to Jack, who has always employed ozone sprayers in all our Garden Fresh facilities, the air in our plants is more than 99 percent free of impurities.

That wasn't the case in the hose of the air gun. Due to the moisture in our production environment, bacteria was building up in the hose, and when the consultant finally got around to checking that, we were shocked by what he found.

"The air in this hose has 30 times the bacteria I'm finding in your outside air. You're literally shooting bacteria all over your onions."

Turns out that air gun was a $60,000 lesson for us. It was immediately retired, although we still have it in our equipment graveyard.

To this day Garden Fresh not only uses fresh onions, but we still peel them by hand, at the rate of over four tons per day. I can't last more than 10 seconds in our vegetable room without my eyes watering.

Also in that vegetable room is a giant centrifuge, into which Jack has our cilantro placed, after washing it three times just to get the water droplets off the leaves. Think of it as the world's largest salad spinner; he did not want the water diluting the flavor profile of our salsa.

One day Jack told us he bought a second centrifuge "just in case the first one breaks." So now our vegetable room has two giant salad spinners.

As our business continued to grow, and as we started to reach out to major national accounts such as Costco, we began to wonder whether we needed to change our manufacturing process. After all, we were still making salsa in five-gallon buckets, just as Jack had done in the back of his restaurant.

So Jack proceeded to bring in the same processing consultants who had helped us with our onion peeling air gun fiasco. They quickly came to the same conclusion: "If you're going to scale nationally you're going to have to use industrial size stainless steel tanks, just like everyone else."

We then bought massive steel tanks, 200, 400, and 600 gallons in size, and began testing our recipes in them.

The problem was, though, that Jack could not get our salsa to taste the same. Onions kept sinking to the bottom of the tanks. The texture of our salsa was different, and the consistency of the product varied widely from container to container.

The process engineers were unrelenting: "This is simply the price you'll have to pay to scale national. You can't expect the same quality from an industrial size batch as you can from a five-gallon bucket. You're not in the back of a restaurant anymore."

We once again reverted to our place in this world for guidance out of this particular dark room. What was the best decision that would enable us to live up to our brand promise?

Jack finally said to the consultants: "I don't care if it impedes our growth, we're not compromising our product. We don't care if we're not the biggest, we just have to be the best."

To this day those industrial size stainless steel tanks are in the same place, our equipment graveyard, with our automatic onion peeling machine and our onion peeling air gun.

And to this day Garden Fresh Gourmet Salsa is made in five-gallon buckets, even though we produce on average more than 75 tons per day. We do so in 38-pound batches, literally by hand, from peeling the onions, coring our green peppers, washing our cilantro three times, then putting it in one of those giant salad spinners, just to get the water droplets off the leaves.

Just after Garden Fresh crossed the $100 million mark, Jack said something very poignant to me: "The proudest thing for me is that the salsa we're making today is the exact same salsa I used to make in the back of my restaurant."

————

FINDING YOUR PLACE IN YOUR CUSTOMERS' WORLD

Just after our Costco L.A. buyer Paul Neumann asked us if we got lost coming out of Texas, he too said some poignant things to Jack and me. He was still holding that pint of Garden Fresh Salsa in his hand: "You know, this just might be the best-packaged salsa I've ever seen."

He then opened the container and tried it. "This is the best fresh salsa I've ever had."

Right before our eyes, Paul validated all the decisions we made with respect to fulfilling our brand promise, to be the best product on the market—in every respect. We had not only found our place in this world, but we were now seeing that fulfilling that commitment was worth it.

Paul continued: "Why is this salsa so much better than everyone else's?

I explained to Paul all that we went through to make our salsa. Peeling onions by hand. Housing two of the world's biggest salad spinners in our vegetable room. Making salsa in five-gallon buckets because we had determined that was the only way for us to truly put the best product on the market.

That even though we were from Detroit, we believed this was the most genuine, authentic salsa in the United States.

Then Jack did something to make Paul realize that the people who were making our products were every bit as genuine and authentic.

As Garden Fresh was growing, Jack and I were traveling to bigger and bigger accounts. We were not exactly hitting the local party stores around our plant anymore. So I told him we needed to upgrade our wardrobes, that it was probably best that he not wear jeans to these buying meetings.

My wife was then working at Neiman Marcus. I sent Jack there, where he bought a pair of $400 pants. He put them on for the first time the morning of our first Costco meeting. We met for breakfast in the hotel lobby prior to heading to Paul's office.

As we were eating, our waitress walked by with a tray of grape smoothies. She subsequently tripped and fell toward Jack, dumping the entire tray onto his new $400 Neiman Marcus trousers.

She was mortified, to say the least—assured that she would lose her job. Broken glass was everywhere, the grape smoothies were all over Jack's new pants.

What she didn't know was that she had dropped that tray of smoothies on the pants of someone who was not only one of the premiere food entrepreneurs in America but also one of the most caring men in America.

Jack at that time couldn't care less about our upcoming huge meeting with Costco, or about his $400 pants. He just wanted to make sure the waitress was OK and would not even think of accepting her apologies. In fact, he eventually left her a $50 tip.

After she had gathered herself, picked up the broken glasses around Jack, and gone back to the kitchen, Jack noticed that the grape smoothies were all over his new pants. He grabbed his cloth napkin, along with mine, and started wiping.

"Wow," he said. "These pants are amazing, the smoothies just wiped clean. There's not even a stain."

On the car ride over Jack still could not get over how easily the smoothies wiped off his new pants: "I guess you really do get what you pay for."

Just after Paul had exclaimed how much he liked our Garden Fresh Gourmet salsa packaging and flavor profile, he offered a suggestion. He wanted us to emphasize that we are an "all natural" salsa to a greater extent on the front of our label and proceeded to tell us just how he'd like us to go about it.

Mid-sentence Jack interrupted Paul to tell him about the smoothie incident and how amazed he was that the whole mess wiped off so easily from his $400 Neiman Marcus pants—even standing up to show Paul there was no stain, and to say how worried he was for that waitress.

Paul was incredulous that he had been interrupted from what, to his credit, was rock-star advice he was in the process of relaying to us. Instead, there's now a 6-foot 5-inch world champion softball player towering over him pointing to a spot on his leg.

So there's Paul just staring at Jack's leg, staring at something that should be there but isn't. No stain. No embedded glass. Nothing.

I'm looking at Jack, saying to myself: "Really, Jack? This? Now?"

But Paul, also to his credit, realized what he had on his hands, that no rational person would interrupt him unless he truly was amazed at the performance of the new pants. Someone who truly was more concerned about the well-being of the waitress than about anything else.

So Paul just sat back and appreciated Jack for what he is, truly genuine. Anything but a slick marketer only concerned about getting onto Paul's shelves, and willing to do so by any means necessary, but instead an authentic guy who truly was more interested in connecting with him on a human level, irrespective of any potential business relationship.

Just as our salsa was genuine and authentic in every manner possible—and in so many ways despite that we were from Detroit.

What was supposed to be an hour-long meeting was an hour and forty-five-minute meeting.

We did get into Costco's L.A. region. Paul Neumann did give us a shot in his deli department. Jack was so excited he told me to find a Mariachi band to play outside of one of Costco's L.A. clubs, but Paul assured me that would not be necessary.

He said: "Just keep making the best salsa I've ever had."

We did just that, and soon took the chain by storm, quickly getting picked up by nine of their ten U.S. and Canadian regions. Today we're in ten out of ten of those regions, an incredibly rare feat for a deli supply company.

———

CREATE MORE VALUE BY MAKING LESS MONEY

I was having dinner one night with the vice president of mergers and acquisitions of a $1 billion public food company who years earlier was interested in purchasing Garden Fresh, but after a year or so of study their board had declined to make an offer.

At dinner I asked: "Now that a few years have passed, what really happened at that board meeting? Why didn't you guys make an offer?"

His first answer was: "The board was worried that you guys are not as profitable as your competitors. Your margins are relatively low, and that concerned us."

He was right. Our gross operating profit margins were slightly below industry standards, but that was largely due to what we go through to make our products and our refusal to cut corners with respect to either our packaging and branding or our flavor profile.

If to be the best we have to peel fresh onions by hand or make salsa in five-gallon buckets, so be it.

We may not be as profitable as our competitors, and thus may not be as valuable in Wall Street's mind, but in my mind we've created more value by ceaselessly committing to our place in this world. By never wavering from the belief that as long as we're the best, there will be a place for us in it.

We embraced what made us special. We were willing to live and die by that.

That's the antithesis of what all our Texas and Southern California–based competitors were doing, producing substandard preservative-based "fresh" salsas with schmaltzy, contrived brands in an attempt to portray themselves as authentic, when in reality they were anything but.

And look where it got us.

Before long Costco became Garden Fresh's largest customer. Today Costco buys almost $20 million worth of Garden Fresh products annually.

Not only is Costco Garden Fresh's number 1 customer, but Garden Fresh is now Costco's number 1 fresh salsa chain-wide.

In the end we blew by each and every one of our competitors. The ones from the Southwest, the ones who had the crazy Tex-Mex themes, just because that's the rational thing to do when you're marketing a fresh salsa. Even though when we started they had ten times the revenue of Garden Fresh, we eventually grew to double their average size.

We eventually got Mike Griffin to join us full time as our chief creative officer. His work was so universally admired we subsequently made him a partner in Garden Fresh Gourmet.

And we never did get that post office box in New Mexico.

Secret 2: Find Your Place

All products and services don't have to be the best in their class. Many companies successfully segment their particular categories. Some offer luxury items or services; some offer value-priced options.

Once you decide what your reason for being is, once you commit to a certain standard for your product or service, you can't deviate from it. Even if that means your labels say you're a fresh salsa company and you're from Detroit.

Even if that means you still have to peel onions by hand. Even if that means you have to make 75 tons of fresh salsa per day in 38-pound batches in five-gallon buckets. Even if that means your margins are lower than your competitors' margins.

Continued

Continued

Embrace what makes you special. Let that serve as your North Star— the guide you look to for direction when you're faced with the difficult, challenging decisions that lie before you. Let that light illuminate the dark rooms you find yourself in.

Once you find your place in this world, and commit to remaining genuine and authentic to the standard you set, the questions you face will answer themselves.

Staying true to that standard will always be your answer.

3

Search for the Holy Grail

"There is no substitute for being in the right industry at the right time."
–*John Chambers, CEO, Cisco, Inc.,* Wall Street Journal
interview, August 9, 2014

So how did Garden Fresh grow from roughly $4 million when I first partnered with Jack and Annette to roughly $104 million in only ten years?

For a bankrupt startup in the food industry, that's shockingly rapid growth.

What was the most critical factor involved?

The answer might surprise you.

For while Annette was right, our products *are* great, I learned a very painful lesson during my lost decade—in those years between the time

I founded American Connoisseur and met Jack at that food show in New York.

Being a great product isn't enough. In fact, far from it.

I can't think of a better example of a great product not being enough than my beloved Mucky Duck Mustard.

On the surface, Mucky Duck has it all.

It differentiates itself on the shelf from other American mustards by being a British pub style mustard.

Its ingredient list is unique. Unlike most American mustards, which consist of simply white vinegar, mustard flour, and turmeric, Mucky Duck is made with cider vinegar, imported mustard flour, real eggs, and sugar. And just as we did at Garden Fresh, I refused the temptation to compromise Mucky Duck's flavor profile by employing less expensive ingredients such as domestic mustard flour and pasteurized eggs.

Its manufacturing process is unique, too, employing a time-sensitive, labor-intensive artisanal method rarely found in mustards. Unlike most American mustards, in which the ingredients are simply whipped together at the point of manufacture and packed cold, Mucky Duck is made over a two-day period and then packed hot.

Its corresponding flavor profile is unlike any other mustard on the market. It doesn't just offer a singular taste, but is more like a journey. At first you experience sweetness, due to the sugar. Then, like a fine wine, a distinct finish takes over and you feel a tangy sensation, the result of the imported mustard flour that gave Mucky Duck a unique, hot flash.

Its name is both meaningful and unforgettable. In England they refer to their local taverns as "Black Swans," and the slang expression for Black Swans is "Mucky Duck." And as I witnessed first-hand for years when I exhibited Mucky Duck at food shows all over North America, people just could not help but smile when they first encountered a mustard called "Mucky Duck."

It had a thoroughly professional label. Just as I had done at Garden Fresh, soon after purchasing Mucky I hired the Eidos Group to redesign the packaging. That was my first experience with our future Garden Fresh Chief Creative Officer Mike Griffin, and to this day I consider what Mike did for Mucky Duck some of his best work.

So just how great is Mucky Duck Mustard?

World Champion great.

There is a World Champion Mustard competition held annually in Napa Valley, California. Typically 500 mustards from eight countries enter. Mucky Duck came in second place in 1995 and was declared World Champion in 1996. Not just for its particular category (Sweet Hot), but it was deemed the best mustard out of the hundreds entered.

To this day I have the World Mustard Championship trophy on display in my office; it weighs more than the Stanley Cup. I was supposed to give it back to the tournament sponsors after a year, but I told them I lost it at a food show. I love the thing and figured possession is nine-tenths of the law.

By virtually any definition Mucky Duck is a great product. You certainly can't do much better than to be World Champion.

But that's not enough.

I eventually learned that mustard is a lousy business to be in.

The mustard market in the United States is small, barely $300 million annually. On top of that, it's barely growing—perhaps at the rate of inflation. If that's not bad enough, the category is completely saturated with hundreds of products, all competing for the same shelf space, which is not only limited but becoming increasingly so. Food retailers are deemphasizing their grocery sections, where most mustard is located. Instead, they are focusing more on expanding their "fresh" food sections that typically line the perimeter of the store, such as meat, seafood, produce, and deli.

Worst of all, mustard is a slow-turn item. The average U.S. household buys mustard only two times per year.

I thought I was onto something with Mucky Duck Mustard. Complete with it's killer packaging and a brand identity marketers would die for. Its unique niche as a British pub-style mustard in a sea of traditional American mustards. Its World Champion pedigree.

I thought I truly had something special on my hands.

But in reality I found myself trapped in a small, saturated, static, slow-turn category. What I was onto was the road to bankruptcy, regardless of how hard I was working or the strategic moves I tried to make.

There's nothing special about that.

About the only market that is worse to find yourself in than mustard is marinades, which is where I originally started, borrowing that $2500 via my then girlfriend/now wife's credit card.

Lucky for me she did not know what we were getting ourselves into either.

More Americans use salad dressings as marinades than use marinades as marinades, and all the same properties that apply to the mustard category are applicable to marinades: relatively small volume, saturated market, slow turns, shrinking shelf space in the center of the store grocery aisles.

Thus, in my esteemed career, which was quickly devolving into a beleaguered career, I was 0–2: first marinades, then mustard.

It's little wonder, then, that I endured a lost decade. Frankly, if I had kept at it and not switched courses it would have been a lost century.

When market forces work against you, it is not going to matter how great your product is.

Instead, it's paramount to respect the characteristics of markets.

And to search for the Holy Grail of American capitalism: find an emerging market, one that is not yet saturated. Then fill that void, that niche, with a great product.

That's exactly what Garden Fresh did. Nothing was as responsible for us adding $100 million in annual revenue in such a relatively short period of time, all in $2 per unit increments.

We did it innocently, at first. But then we did so by design.

HOLY GRAIL I

For decades ketchup reigned as the number one condiment in America, but in the early 1990s salsa overtook it as the Mexican food craze took hold.

But for the most part, nearly all the salsa that was being sold in this country was the shelf-stable variety found in the grocery aisle merchandised alongside tortilla chips. It was salsa that was pasteurized, via heat, cooked at 180 degrees for 10 seconds to kill all the food-borne pathogens such as mold, yeast, and bacteria, then packed while still hot in a jar, and sealed with a metal lid.

In effect it was a "canned" product, in the traditional sense of the word—just what your grandmother used to do to preserve food in the height of the Depression.

And it had a 13-month shelf life. At least.

About the only place you could find "fresh" salsa, in other words salsa that had not been cooked, was in the refrigerated deli service counter in your local supermarket. The deli manager would make a bowl of pico de gallo–style diced tomato salsa every morning with soon-to-expire tomatoes and onions that the produce manager would send over. You'd then order it the same way you would fresh potato salad or coleslaw, with the woman behind the counter scooping it into a plastic container, lidding it and selling it to you by weight.

It had a three-to-five-day shelf life. At most.

By the mid-1990s, though, small food manufacturers starting making and packaging fresh salsa on their own and selling it to supermarkets that would offer it in their deli departments.

These new fresh salsas, professionally manufactured, had a 45- to 60-day shelf life.

Deli department buyers welcomed it, as it was a way for them to offer a fresh variation on what was now the number one condiment in the country, salsa, something they were never able to do with ketchup.

Salsa in general had become king of all condiments, and fresh salsa was something new and something American consumers were willing to try, as it was perceived to be an attempt to elevate the salsa experience from what was being offered in their grocery sections.

It was an emerging category.

And that's the category Jack Aronson stumbled into when he pulled out that five-gallon bucket in the back of that small restaurant and came up with a world-class recipe for fresh salsa. In 15 minutes. All in an attempt to be able to pay his electric bill.

It's sometimes better to be lucky than be good. And, luckily, what a category fresh salsa turned out to be.

As opposed to mustard, which was completely saturated, there were virtually no national brands occupying the fresh salsa space when Jack thought to pull out that five-gallon bucket.

As opposed to mustard, which is traditionally featured in the shrinking center grocery aisles of the supermarket, fresh salsa was merchandised in the ever-hot, rapidly growing perimeter of the store. In the deli.

Also, as opposed to mustard, which is low turn, with the average U.S. household buying it only two times a year, consumers go through salsa like water. The average Garden Fresh customer consumes two units of our fresh salsa per week.

In other words, Jack found the Holy Grail: an emerging market that was not yet saturated. Or perhaps more appropriately, the Holy Grail found him.

Regardless, we proceeded, with our great product, which we fought so hard to keep great, to revolutionize the fresh salsa category — eventually becoming the dominant national brand.

But none of that would have happened without the stars being aligned, in terms of market characteristics, to the extent they were with fresh salsa. It was a rapidly growing category without substantial competition. It was ripe for a truly great product to come along and disrupt it.

If Jack had devoted that same 15 minutes to develop a new marinade, as I had done, or a new mustard, a category I entered by purchasing Mucky Duck, he'd still be a struggling restaurateur.

And I'd still be selling life insurance at night trying to make ends meet.

But while Jack unwittingly found Garden Fresh's first Holy Grail, we purposely sought after and identified many others.

HOLY GRAIL 2

By the year 2000, hummus, the Mediterranean chickpea spread, started showing up in high-end supermarket delis, particularly on the east and west coasts. The trend soon spread throughout the country.

By the middle of the decade, hummus had not only overtaken fresh salsa nationally in total sales but was continuing to grow faster as a category than fresh salsa.

Thus, hummus was yet another Holy Grail, and the quintessential one at that: an emerging market, not yet saturated, without a high-quality, dominant national brand.

I told Jack and our board this was a category we needed to enter. We eventually purchased a metro Detroit hummus company and shortly thereafter launched our own line of Garden Fresh Hummus. But not before following our North Star and ensuring that our hummus was the very best on the market.

Most hummus in the United States is made with canned chickpeas. At the point of manufacture, the can is opened and dumped into a mixer with hummus' other primary ingredients, namely water, salt, garlic, and ground sesame paste, known as tahini.

If you want a truly world-class hummus, however, you need to employ the authentic, ancient Mediterranean method. Instead of using canned chickpeas, you use dried chickpeas that are roasted, whipped into a mash, and cured overnight.

The next day, at the point of manufacture, rather than just open a can of chickpeas, you employ this mash you made the day before.

It's time- and labor-intensive, but if you want the best hummus in the world, it's what you have to do.

The metro Detroit company that we purchased used canned chickpeas. That was not in alignment with our Garden Fresh values brand promise, to be the best. Jack subsequently went to Israel and came back with $1.9 million worth of equipment so that we could make the best hummus on the market.

We proceeded to develop a great line of hummus, launching it under our Garden Fresh Gourmet label in the first quarter of 2007.

Today that Garden Fresh Gourmet line of hummus is the fifth largest brand in the United States.

As the Mediterranean diet grew increasingly popular in this country, fresh hummus grew right along with it, almost exponentially. Similarly, Garden Fresh's hummus business has grown right along with that, so much so that if the current trends continue, within a couple years we may be selling as much hummus as we do fresh salsa.

Due to the hummus we make for major national retailers, in addition to the hummus we make for our own labels, Garden Fresh is now the third-largest hummus manufacturer in America.

————

HOLY GRAIL 3

The hummus we make for major national retailers involves a concept known as private label.

Retailers have made the strategic decision to differentiate themselves by developing their own brands — brands that can only be found in their stores, not in their competitors' stores.

The concept is not new; private labels have always been around. But in the past, retailers positioned them as commodities and packaged them in pedestrian black-and-white labels that typically had the lowest prices in their respective categories.

What modern day retailers are doing, however, is upgrading the standards of their private label programs, moving them from commodity-oriented lines to lines that match or exceed the national brand, both in terms of flavor profile and packaging.

Are they the exact same product? Not really.

Major U.S. food retailers are taking their private label programs so seriously they're hiring their own corporate chefs, and very often these chefs fly into Detroit to meet with us at our Garden Fresh production facilities.

What they experience often astonishes them. The largest manufacturer of fresh salsa in the United States not making their product in 5000-pound batches in a 400-gallon tank, but rather in 38-pound batches in five-gallon buckets.

Thus, when they want another onion added to the recipe they don't order it and wait for us to make an industrial size batch when we can find time in our production schedule to do so. Or have us make what is known as a "bench sample" on a counter. Good luck trying to convert that to a massive production scale; it never tastes the same.

Instead, with Garden Fresh they get a true production batch, literally within minutes, as all we have to do is add another onion to that five-gallon bucket, mix it, and voilá their vision is instantly realized. They can immediately taste it to see if that is indeed what they're looking for.

Private label was also a significant Holy Grail that propelled our growth.

It was an emerging category, as the U.S. food market was moving from approximately 20 percent private label to close to 30 percent today. Many industry experts believe it will one day comprise 40 percent of the total food market in this country. In Europe private label programs already make up almost 45 percent of all food sold.

Garden Fresh embraced the private label phenomenon occurring in this country. Coupling that with our commitment to quality ensured that major retailers embraced us as well.

Within five years, private label programs comprised just over 30 percent of our total Garden Fresh business.

INFINITE HOLY GRAILS

Holy Grails are elusive, but they are out there.

In the food industry there is a wonderful dynamic at work that seems to spontaneously generate them.

Americans are not only open to trying new products, but we search for them. That can't be said of every nation on Earth. I've had several people from Europe, for example, say something along the lines of "You Americans are wonderful; you'll try anything. We're too set in our ways in Europe, too bound by tradition."

Sure enough, it seems like every decade something new pops onto the American food scene and makes its way into our collective cultural DNA. In the 1970s it was specialty mustards (think Grey Poupon) and wine (think Mondavi). In the 1980s it was olive oil. In the 1990s it was new age drinks (think Snapple), plus the emergence of bottled water.

And sure enough, that happened again in the 2000s with both Greek yogurt and hummus.

I was 20 years too late with my specialty mustard, Mucky Duck, and I was probably a half-century too late with my American Connoisseur Marinades.

Garden Fresh, however, has always been in sync with market forces, market forces that were working for us, where the wind was at our back propelling us forward and forgiving us for the many mistakes we were making. Not market forces that were working against us where the wind was blowing in our faces compounding the many mistakes we were making.

In the end, Garden Fresh found three Holy Grails that were primarily responsible for our growth. First with fresh salsa, then with hummus, and finally with the private label revolution.

There are Holy Grails in every industry. Savor one when you find it, but ignore it at your peril. I speak from personal experience when I say there's no surer way to a lost decade than to ignore the characteristics of the market you are entering.

Secret 3: What's Your Holy Grail?

There is a reason why more than 90 percent of all new businesses fail.

It's not because they were not based on great new products or services.

It's because too many people don't realize that being great isn't enough.

Because too many people don't respect the characteristics of the markets they're entering.

Is my market saturated? Is it already so crowded that any offering, no matter how great, will not even be noticed, let alone gain traction?

Is my product or service a "me too" item, even though it may be great in and of itself?

This Holy Grail instructs us to first look for markets that are emerging, that are not yet saturated, *then develop a great product,* and the world will indeed beat a path to your door.

When you do build a better mousetrap, you'll realize another benefit. You'll find that the world will be much more forgiving, will tolerate your mistakes, will be much more patient as you sort through your growing pains.

The world simply has to do that. It has no other choice. Your great product will only be available from a limited number of people.

Make sure you're one of those people.

Would you like to spend significantly less time in the dark room? Then encounter less drama and fewer hardships when you're in there?

Then first search for and identify the Holy Grail before you take that first step.

4

Never Sell Anything

"He's liked, but he's not—well liked."

—Death of a Salesman, *Arthur Miller*

Jack, Annette, and I had entered the dark room. Several of them. We had found our place in this world and did all we could to live up to the promises we believed Garden Fresh should stand for—to be the best products in our categories. We had stumbled into finding our first Holy Grail, then searched and found others.

All that resulted in rapid growth. During the first six years of our partnership, in fact, we grew at an average annual rate of 50 percent.

That put us at roughly the size of our competitors, in the neighborhood of $50 million in annual sales.

What put us so far ahead of our competitors, resulting in Garden Fresh eventually growing to twice their average size, to $110 million in annual sales?

It was our unique, almost unheard of approach to market, an approach in which we resisted the temptation to enter into mere transactional relationships with our accounts. One in which we simply offered our products and they simply submitted purchase orders.

An approach that on the surface seems irrational. Just like salsa from Detroit itself.

It was an approach in which we committed to *never selling anything*.

Instead, we strove for something deeper. More genuine. More authentic.

We strove to become *true strategic partners with our customers*.

To us being true strategic partners meant we were not just in business to sell whatever we happened to be making. Rather, we existed to grow our buyers' business. Our mission was not to make short-term transactions but to establish a long-term relationship in which we solved their problems—problems both known and unknown to them. One in which we became a part of their lives. One in which we advanced their careers.

Our approach of never "selling" anything but instead forming strategic partnerships is as responsible for Garden Fresh's success as anything else we did.

I have had countless buyers over the years reinforce this notion. Buyers from the largest retailers in this country told me, unsolicited, that their experience with Garden Fresh was unlike any other they had with other vendors they had dealt with.

We'd hear it all the time: "You guys are just different." "No one else is like you." "More companies need to do this."

Our approach worked. Spectacularly. Not because it was some contrived scheme, but because it was simply the right thing to do.

Here's how we did it. How we grew to be double the size of our competitors without selling anything.

THIS NEEDS TO BE FROM THE HEART

I would love to say our approach initially was a premeditated, calculated textbook decision in which we believed we could be more profitable in the long run by never selling anything. In reality, it emanated more from the heart than anything else.

I was always so grateful to our buyers for taking a chance on us, these two guys from Detroit who were making salsa, of all things. Helping these people whom I honestly felt indebted to was the least I could do to return the favor.

We just wanted to do all we could for them, as a token of our appreciation and gratitude for featuring Garden Fresh as much as for any rational business profit maximization model. So our approach resulted in us doing more for them than their average, ordinary supplier would typically do.

That spirit stayed with us, even as we grew. To this day we genuinely care about our buyers, both personally and professionally. In fact, I'm disappointed if, over time, I don't come to think of buyers as friends, as people I'd like to keep in touch with once they move off the desk I'm working with them on.

It makes a difference. Customers can tell whether you're rooting for them, truly, or if you're just there to advance your own cause. If you're going to form a partnership with someone, your heart simply has to be in the right place.

BUILD RESPECT, GENUINELY

The term "selling" often has a negative connotation, often deservedly so; it's a demeaning process for everyone involved.

"Selling" is trying to convince someone to purchase something whether it is in his best interests or not. It is, of course, in your best interests, but if you're not addressing a specific need of a customer, selling devolves into a coercive exercise designed to enrich yourself at the expense of someone else, either one of your competitors or your customer, who might be better off with someone else's product.

Why do people fear dealing with the stereotypical used car salesman? Because they assume there's a lack of integrity involved, that the salesman just wants to move the used car off his lot, for as much money as possible.

That's precisely why, although most salesman are pleasant by definition and liked (you're never going to purchase something from someone you can't stand being in the same room with, after all), they're not *well* liked.

They're not *well* liked because they're not respected, not respected as someone who sincerely wants the best outcome for his or her customer. Not respected because there is subtext involved in the relationship and what's transpiring on the surface—what the salesperson is saying—is radically different from what is actually occurring.

He's saying the car is great and that it will be perfect for you. What is actually happening is that he's trying to move the car off his lot. He does not know if the car is great and does not care if is perfect for you or not. His own interests trump those of his customer.

In this context "selling" is a manipulative exercise.

It's no way to build a strategic partnership.

Even worse than trying to manipulate someone is to be the one being manipulated.

Strategic partnerships rest on a foundation of respect, not where the salesperson is searching for "angles" in which to maximize revenue. Rise above the natural temptation to do that. . . to "sell." In the long run you'll create far greater value for everyone involved if you strike up a true partnership.

DON'T BE AFRAID TO BE UNPREPARED

One thing we don't do is research an account or "Google" a buyer prior to a meeting.

Some may believe this seeming lack of preparation is lazy. We, however, always want to learn about a company and a buyer and his or her experiences directly from the people, in their own words. Not from some recently published article which may be right or wrong, and which may color our views of the company ahead of time. We'd rather go in completely open-minded with respect to the situation, as a blank slate, and let them paint their own canvass for us. We feel that if they agreed to meet with us we owe them at least that.

When I'm meeting with someone offering me a product or service, I'm often struck by how they'll ask me a question and then proceed to answer it based on research they've done on me—literally finishing my sentences before I can.

On the surface I ask myself: "How genuine is this question if the answer is already known? Is this a game?"

Deep down, I feel violated. It's unsettling to think of someone looking into your past so that he can sell more to you.

Don't think you can research your way into knowing a customer or a customer's situation better than he knows it himself.

Don't be afraid to learn about your customer's needs directly.

WHAT YOU DON'T BRING TO A MEETING IS AS IMPORTANT AS WHAT YOU DO BRING

Our customers are often more astonished at what we don't bring to a meeting as opposed to what we do bring.

First, I never bring the attitude that I absolutely *need* to make a deal. If I can't genuinely meet a buyer's needs to a greater extent than any of our competitors can, I'm comfortable walking out empty-handed. That's just not what I'm there for; that's not how strategic partnerships are formed.

Another thing we don't do is to walk in with a brochure or a sell sheet or a leave-behind.

Sales materials such as these are incredibly pedestrian. Every company develops them; thus, you're not exactly distinguishing yourself by opening or closing a meeting by handing one to your buyer. In fact, the opposite is true; you're actually distinguishing yourself from your competitors by not having one.

Worse yet, they're not genuine. Sales brochures, by nature, are designed to put the company in the best possible light. Buyers certainly know that, so they don't take them seriously.

By extension, we don't believe we're taken seriously if we walk in with such an obvious tool of self-promotion.

They're manipulative in nature. They announce right off the bat that you're there to "sell" something. That what is about to ensue is a typical "sales process." That being open and honest with your customer is something that will have to wait.

Another thing we don't do to our buyers is dump a massive amount of data in their laps.

We realize the current business zeitgeist suggests making purely data-driven decisions. We reject that notion, particularly in meetings with our buyers.

Data is important, but only to a certain extent. We use it only to be able to talk intelligently about what's going on in our industry, from the 65,000-foot level.

On the surface, too often data is just another form of manipulation.

Most food companies with a national presence rely on a Chicago-based company, Information Resources Incorporated (IRI). For a fee IRI provides national, scientifically gathered and disseminated sales data for every item sold in supermarkets and groups them together by category.

Thus, at any time any company can purchase data and see where their products rank in any given region, and/or nationally, in comparison to their competitors.

Most food companies with a national presence march their sales force into meetings with buyers armed with reams of sales data, extolling their products' performance in the marketplace.

While on the surface IRI numbers are objective, how they're viewed is subjective—and highly so at that.

It's incredibly easy to manipulate the data to suit your company's or product's particular point of view.

Buyers recognize data interpretation for what it is, just another sales tool used by companies to try to influence them to purchase your product or service. No company sends their salespeople into meetings with data that is not in their best interests to present, that does not paint their products' sales in the best light possible.

It's the digital equivalent of the glossy sales brochure. Yet another form of manipulation that's being foisted on a buyer, in the form of a spreadsheet, and a mind-numbing one at that, filled with seemingly endless numbers, laid out in a style-less, soul-less fashion.

While data-driven decision making is all the rage in the modern business world, in our experience buyers still want to rely on their instincts. About the only data they truly trust is their own internally generated sales data, in other words, what is actually moving off *their* shelves.

And the best buyers want to exercise their own judgment with respect to what they put on their shelves. They still want to rely on their instincts, on their guts, as much as anything else.

Therefore, we at Garden Fresh don't use IRI data in our meetings with buyers, even though, as the number 1 brand of fresh salsa by sales nationally, no one has a better story to communicate than we do. There can only be one brand that can claim to lead the nation in sales, so you'd think the brand that does, Garden Fresh, would relentlessly pound that fact into a buyer's head.

I'm struck by how often buyers will thank me, at the end of our meeting, for not dumping huge amounts of data on them and making them sift through it all, just looking at a sea of numbers on a spreadsheet and listening to how we as a company spin it in our favor.

I even had one buyer, at a major east coast supermarket chain, bring a 73-page hard copy PowerPoint presentation into one of our meetings.

"Do you know what this is?" she asked me.

"I have no idea," I responded.

"This is what one of your largest competitors handed to me yesterday, just as our meeting started. I said to him: 'What the hell is this? I don't have time to go through all this.' He told me not to worry, he'd walk me through it on his laptop. I told him I didn't have time for that either. The only reason I didn't throw this in my wastepaper basket right after the meeting is because I wanted to show it to you, because I knew you'd never do something like this to me."

We feel that would be less than genuine—disrespectful, even—to the extent that it fundamentally violates the foundation of a strategic partnership.

The result of that meeting with that major east coast supermarket chain? She dropped our competitor's salsa line and brought in Garden Fresh. Exclusively.

YOUR CUSTOMERS NEED TO SEE YOUR C-SUITE

So I never walk into a meeting having researched an account or a buyer or with canned sales materials or brochures, or with reams of data manipulated to support my position.

But I do walk in with my Garden Fresh business card.

A funny thing happened shortly after I became a partner. Prior to my becoming a partner I'd walk in with my vice president of sales card and would receive a predictably polite response.

Shortly after formally partnering with Jack and Annette, though, I assumed the title of vice chairman, and the response I received from buyers was demonstrably different.

Suddenly, I was no longer just a run-of-the-mill regional sales manager, or even just another VP of sales. Instead, I was a principal of the firm, someone integrally involved in both building and running the company.

While I viewed myself as I always had, I was being treated differently by buyers. More respectfully, both in terms of their tone and attitude, even in their posture while sitting behind their desks.

As a result it became easier, and more natural, for us to have a strategic conversation regarding how our respective companies might complement each other and how Garden Fresh might be able to help in our buyer's particular circumstance.

It demonstrated to me how important it is for C-suite level executives to be involved in the sales process.

There's an old maxim that suggests the president of a company should walk through the floor of his plant every day, just to get a feel for what is really going on, how morale is, what issues might be occurring that are not being conveyed to his level.

It's important for the employees to know that their efforts are at the very least being acknowledged and, one hopes, appreciated beyond that by the leadership of the company.

The same is true for the revenue generating side of business. If you truly want to form strategic partnerships with your customers, the executives involved in formulating the strategy for your own company need to be in front of your customer base to the greatest extent possible.

Just as it's important to employees to be acknowledged by the leaders of their company, it's important to buyers that the leaders of the companies they're purchasing from are working with them.

In Garden Fresh's case, that C-suite exec walking the floor of our plants every day was Jack, and the C-suite exec involved in the sales process was me.

During our six-year period of 50 percent annual sales increases, about the only thing we did to control our growth was something we actually *didn't* do: establish a formal sales team. We were having so much trouble keeping up with demand that hiring more people to sell what we couldn't produce anyway just never seemed to make much sense.

Typically, a company our size would divide the country into five to eight regions with sales reps embedded in each reporting into a national sales manager anchored to a desk in the home office.

That was never really in the cards for Garden Fresh. In the early part of our partnership, Jack and I often traveled together making sales calls. As our company grew, our roles became increasingly silo'd, with me running around the country putting deals together and Jack getting all that product out the door, essentially handling operations. We shared strategy details.

We still don't have much of a sales force. Currently, Garden Fresh's top ten customers comprise almost 90 percent of our revenue, and I personally handle eight of them.

I can't say that's advisable for every $100 million company. By me meeting with virtually every one of the top ten retailers in the country, though, I knew more about our categories, from a national perspective, than any of the buyers I was meeting with.

Of course, the buyers I was dealing with knew more about their particular situations than I did, but I knew what their competitors were doing, as well as the strengths and weaknesses of just about every major deli program in the country.

I never violate anyone's trust or confidence. I've never told a buyer that "Your competitor X is doing this and you should respond accordingly," but I did almost by osmosis develop a holistic view of the deli supply business in North America that no one else any of our buyers would meet with could match.

That holistic overview, that category expertise, became a valuable resource to our accounts.

But to expect a regional sales manager to command that level of respect with a buyer is unrealistic. Accounts look to C-suite level executives for strategic guidance, strategic guidance both from an industry perspective and with respect to one's own company.

As a Garden Fresh C-suite level executive, I was intimately familiar with our capabilities. Our pricing structure. Our margin guidelines. Our capacity.

As a result I could talk intelligently about what programs we could realistically put together, and how soon. What we could truly make happen together. I never had to say I had to check with the home office and see what I could do. I *was* the home office.

Only a C-suite level executive is going to garner the level of attention needed to unlock the creative juices of a buyer and begin the process of true value creation.

Only a C-suite level executive can form true strategic partnerships.

OFFER YOUR COMPANY, NOT YOUR PRODUCTS

There's another aspect of our approach of never selling anything that's counterintuitive, even irrational.

At Garden Fresh we commit ourselves to making the best products on the market. Our retail customers merchandise them on their shelves. Our consumers buy them—to the tune of a million per week.

Yet in our meetings with our buyers we don't focus on those products.

Instead we focus on our company.

It's more important that we establish who we are and what makes us special. What our capabilities are. Our goal is for our customers to have a long-term relationship with *us*, not necessarily with one or any number of our products.

I'll bring samples into our meetings, but more often than not I won't open them for buyers to try. I don't want them to feel pressured to comment on them in front of me. I'd rather respect their privacy and let them taste in the comfort of their personal time so they can truly concentrate on what they're tasting.

I'm confident that when buyers do taste our Garden Fresh line they'll experience the "wow" factor that keeps consumers buying them over and over again. In my time with them, though, I want them to experience the "wow" factor of the story and the people and the company that makes those products in the first place.

I do this in the form of a PowerPoint presentation.

Now the last thing the business world needs is another PowerPoint presentation. But our approach is different, to say the least—counterintuitive, but this time in a rational sense.

First, we never, absolutely never, print out the slides and give them to anyone who might be in the room. Buyers are always being handed large stacks of paper from people they meet with, and then are expected to follow along, flipping pages in precise concert with the salesperson.

I'd never dream of asking a buyer to try to listen to me while simultaneously try to figure out what page I'm on.

At the same time, buyers are human; if they don't find one particular page compelling they'll start flipping forward. Suddenly, you're talking about one aspect of your company and they're a few pages ahead of you reading about another.

The result is a jumbled, at best, and certainly incoherent message, one that you're not in control of.

What we do, then, is to prepare a digital PowerPoint, then present it on a laptop computer, equipped with a remote that allows me to advance the slides from a distance.

Thus, I'm controlling and dictating both the message and its pace. The buyer and I are, figuratively (since I never hand him or her a physical presentation), on the same page.

Then there's the PowerPoint presentation itself.

Our Garden Fresh Chief Creative Officer, Mike Griffin, has a brilliantly effective approach to creating PowerPoint presentations. He refers to it as speaker support.

Speaker support PowerPoint dictates that any slide that comes up in a presentation should only serve as an illustration for what the narrator is talking about. The presenting party should convey the information, but the slide itself never should.

Thus, you'll never see in a Garden Fresh presentation data-centric slides, commonly known as "eye charts"—slides so filled with information you feel like you are in the midst of a visit with your ophthalmologist.

Similarly, you'll never see bullet points employed in a Garden Fresh presentation, and certainly not multiple bullet points.

I'm amazed when I'm on the receiving end of a PowerPoint presentation and someone puts up a slide with anywhere from six to eight bullet points on it, then just reads them. I always just skim through them, leaping ahead until I find one that's interesting, but rarely am I still tuned in to what the speaker is saying. He's on one bullet point and I'm on another.

Similarly, when a slide comes up with multiple graphs, often accompanied by more bullet points, I skim ahead.

These are often accompanied by the speaker pointing to the screen and saying "as you can plainly see."

In reality the audience can't plainly see anything.

No one can effectively read one thing on a screen and simultaneously listen to anyone describe what it all means.

I once met with an executive from a billboard company who told me the most effective billboards are the ones that actually say the least, in which the marketers have distilled their message down to it's essence and only employ four to six words or a simple symbol to convey their point of view.

He told me he meets with companies who come to him with thick binders housing statistics derived from innumerable focus groups. They insist five or six messages, not simply words, but sales points or product attributes, must be included on the billboard. All because their precious research told them so.

Common sense would tell you that if you say too much to a passing motorist, in reality you say nothing at all... that sometimes less truly is more.

He challenged me to start paying attention as I'm driving and that I'd see what he was talking about. Sure enough, to this day I do that, and it's incredible how much information some companies try to cram onto billboards, completely ignoring that a driver only has maybe two to three seconds to actually pay attention to it.

I've always taken that advice, and the subsequent experience, to heart. Thus, the slides in a Garden Fresh PowerPoint presentation are designed like the most effective billboards you can possibly imagine. Clean and simple, simply reflecting what I might be talking about at the time.

When I'm describing Garden Fresh's innocent origins, founded in the back of a small 1200-square-foot restaurant just outside of Detroit, up pops a shot of the actual restaurant, Jack's old Clubhouse Bar-B-Q.

When I'm talking about how we still make our salsa in five-gallon buckets, all you'll see on the slide is a five-gallon bucket.

The effect is as if you're watching TV, just looking at shots on the screen while a narrator tells you a story.

While some may say that all a company would have to do, then, is to prepare a video and play that for a buyer, that would require a one-size-fits-all approach.

Prior to each meeting, Mike and I prepare a specific PowerPoint presentation tailored to the particular account I'll be meeting with. I include aspects that I believe will be important to them and delete things that won't apply to them.

Similarly, during the presentation, I may talk more about certain aspects of our company that pertain to them and less about others.

No video can possibly offer that kind of flexibility. Videos are essentially electronic brochures and can't possibly be taken as seriously as our approach to formally introducing our company.

———•———

DON'T SUGGESTIVE SELL; SUGGESTIVE PARTNER

Our Garden Fresh presentation details who we are, where we came from, and what our capabilities are. It's a heartfelt rendering of our *story*, and about what we believe makes us special, all unfolding in a conversational tone.

Being in such a position enables me to take the term "suggestive selling" to a new level.

Go into any fast-food restaurant and order something to eat and the person behind the counter will almost always ask whether you'd like to add to your order: "Would you like fries or a drink with that burger?"

That's suggestive selling, on a minor league level. I never like being on the receiving end of it, as to me it's insulting. If I had wanted fries or a drink with my burger, I would have ordered it.

But what offering our company instead of our products does is elevate suggestive selling to a strategically superior position—to suggestive partnering.

From that foundation, we'll have a conversation regarding what Garden Fresh can do go grow his or her business. Not simply by offering a specific product or line, but instead by taking a holistic overview of the category and exploring where we can be of service.

I'm in this for the long run. I'm not so concerned about how a buyer feels about our current products. If he or she likes them, great, but if not we'll take our unique approach to food production and tailor something to meet his or her specific needs. In fact, moving forward I'll be disappointed if in some way, shape, or form we don't do just that, create something special together somewhere down the road.

For that to happen, he or she needs to know who he's dealing with, not what products he or she is currently dealing with.

Thus, we'd simply rather represent ourselves as the premiere fresh salsa manufacturer in North American and offer to tailor a program employing our five-gallon bucket micro-batch process to meet this particular buyer's needs.

If he or she wants our salsa a certain way or wants a unique variety using some ingredient that is indigenous to his region, we're happy to do that.

The same is true for pricing. If we have to tailor a particular product or program to meet certain pricing criteria, we're happy to explore those options as well.

While Garden Fresh may have grown to be one of the largest companies in our space, we've never lost the ability to be incredibly adaptive and responsive, to an unprecedented degree, to our customer's needs.

It's not one-size-fits-all for us. It's the antithesis of that.

MELT AWAY THE SKEPTICISM

Few if any companies follow this approach to sales or adapt this counterintuitive notion of not selling anything but instead forming genuine, strategic partnerships with their customers.

I know that by how so many of the buyers I meet with are skeptical, and noticeably so, when I first enter their offices. Too many salespeople are still trying to manipulate them, to "sell" them something, whether it's in their best interests or not. They're naturally defensive with me, assuming Garden Fresh is just a typical run-of-the-mill supplier that will say anything to get on their shelves.

That skepticism almost always melts away by the end of the meeting, because during the meeting they've been treated like human beings and not subjected to a dehumanizing sales process.

No glossy sales brochures. No one who has violated their privacy by "Googleing" their life story ahead of time. No one dumping a pile of paper in front of them, filled with data that may or not be accurate but certainly is manipulated to the benefit of the salesman's interests, and then asking them to follow along page after page while they ramble through it all. No one pushing one-size-fits-all products and pricing. No one pushing them to try some samples if they're not ready to. No one pushing for a sale at the end.

Instead, they receive a presentation detailing a remarkable only-in-America story and about the people behind it. About what they have gone through to ensure the products they're making are the exact same product as a 44-year-old bankrupt chef just outside of Detroit did when he pulled out a five-gallon bucket and made the best salsa he could, which just so happens to now be the best-selling salsa in the country.

That's followed up by a strategic conversation with one of the principals of the company, someone who treats them like a friend, about how Garden Fresh might be able to grow their business, both in the short term and in the long run.

Because we're there to partner with them. On a strategic basis.

The difference between the moment I walk into the office and when I walk out is palpable. Their understandable cynicism is gone; they have just experienced something they're not accustomed to, something refreshing.

The same is true of our relationship moving forward; it's not the typical vendor relationship.

Once buyers trust us, they treat us differently. Once we earn their respect, a collaborative process ensues, one in which they'll reach out to us with a project or idea almost as often as I'll contact them with something new we're working on.

Time after time, the largest retailers in North America reach out to Garden Fresh, unsolicited, to meet their needs.

Now this approach to revenue generation will not work over time without insanely great products—I'm not exactly walking into these meetings with dog food. It's not lost on me that at the end of the day I have the best packaged, best tasting products in my industry.

But even with these advantages, it's not a given that we would get on the shelves of as many major national retailers as we have. From there our business would never have grown to the extent it has without us having formed true strategic partnerships with our customers, to the extent that we were having so much trouble keeping up with production we barely ever got around to hiring a sales force.

The age of the wheeler-dealer is over.

Buyers need problems solved, and when they seek solutions they're going to reach out to their strategic partners, not the glorified used car salesman who just happened to get a job in their industry.

Not to someone who is simply trying to sell them something.

They'd much rather work with someone who never sells them anything.

Secret 4: Ready to Stop Selling?

It sounds crazy, this notion that you'll sell more if you never sell at all.

But the business world is becoming increasingly sophisticated. In turn, your company's approach to market needs to distinguish itself from the sea of sameness your customers are experiencing. To advance to the next level.

To the level of strategic partnering with your customers.

Ask yourself whether your interests are truly in alignment with your customers, both personally and professionally.

Take a heartfelt approach to your customers, one in which you genuinely care for their well-being, just as you would for a friend.

Remember that even worse than trying to manipulate someone is to be the one being manipulated.

Practice the art of being unprepared. By not researching your customer's life story ahead of time, just to gain some sort of advantage. By not walking in with sales brochures or data that has only been manipulated to advance your own cause.

Recognize that your buyers are looking for industry expertise in general and institutional knowledge in particular.

Continued

Continued

The senior leaders of your company must be involved in the formation of strategic partnerships, then offer your company's capabilities, not just your products.

Once your interests are in complete alignment with your customers' interests, you'll be in a position to elevate your approach to them.

Not to amateurishly suggestive *sell to* them, but instead to professionally suggestive *partner with* them.

It makes a difference. The key is to realize it has to make a difference for both you and your customer. Not just for you.

5

Build a Company Woody Allen Would Be Proud Of

"80 percent of life is showing up."

— Woody Allen

At Garden Fresh we adopted the approach to never "sell" anything. Instead we committed to something more aspirational: to form true strategic partnerships with our customers.

Just as we adopted a strategic approach to building relationships with our **customers**, though, we also adopted a strategic approach to building our **company**.

One in which our sales force did not have to "sell" to be effective.

One in which about all they had to do to be successful was show up.

Show up and simply have conversations with our customers, conversations in which we outlined our capabilities instead of talking our product line up, conversations in which we asked questions to learn about our customers' needs.

We'd listen, then shape a program via our customers' words, to the extent that a true long-term strategic partnership would naturally, almost inevitably, ensue.

To be able to do that we had to layer into our program more strategic advantages than anyone else in our industry had. Advantages our competitors could not possibly match. That customers could only get from Garden Fresh.

It is the sales force's responsibility to first secure, then "show up" for the meeting. To have the conversations with their customers.

It is the responsibility of a company's senior management to ensure that, when they do show up, they have more arrows in their quiver than anyone else the customer will meet.

And those conversations would include not only being able to meet our buyers' immediate and apparent needs, but also needs they did not even know they had.

We viewed it as our responsibility to bring to the table innovations that the person sitting on the other side of the table might not even be aware of.

To get to that point, where we would be uniquely qualified to meet our buyers' needs, both known and unknown, we relentlessly kept adding features to our overall program that no one else in our industry could counter.

It wasn't always this way. In the beginning, Jack and I would show up merely hoping our buyers would give two flunkies from Detroit peddling a fresh salsa line a chance, as strange and incoherent as that might sound.

We certainly were not above sympathy sales—and we certainly got more than our fair share of them.

But it wasn't long before we realized we needed to be more than that, even as great as our salsa was, even as irrationally persistent as we were in getting our products to our growing customer base.

So shortly into our partnership we made a strategic pivot, deciding that we wanted Garden Fresh to be more than a fresh salsa company. We wanted Garden Fresh to be a full service deli supply company—one that the country had never seen the likes of before.

Doing so took time, but we began layering one strategic advantage after another into our overall program, building Garden Fresh into a company that had competitive advantages that no one else in our industry possessed.

COMPETITIVE ADVANTAGE 1: WE'RE THE NUMBER 1 BRAND OF FRESH SALSA IN THE UNITED STATES

Strategic Benefit: There can only be one "#1" brand of anything in any category. Once Garden Fresh became the largest brand of fresh salsa in America, it became something we and only we could claim, something we and only we can offer that our customers could get from us.

COMPETITIVE ADVANTAGE 2: GARDEN FRESH DIPS

I had just met with a buyer at one of our largest accounts; he asked if I could develop a line of Garden Fresh dips. He was having trouble finding the quality he was looking for and thought our small batch, artisanal approach would do the trick.

I told him I'd be happy to. After discussing with him how many varieties he was looking for, what price point he wanted to hit, and what his business model was, I approached Jack with the idea.

I didn't have to ask Jack twice.

To provide as many people as possible with incredibly great food is Jack's inherent, unspoken mission in life. It's why he originally gravitated to the restaurant business. Cooking was a means for Jack to give a gift to someone, and for a man as giving as Jack it's important to be able to do so on a daily basis. Running a restaurant provided him with a vehicle to do just that.

Nothing illustrates how giving Jack was, in this sense, than his old Clubhouse BBQ restaurant menu; it had 93 items on it.

I know not by counting but because Jack had them numbered, right there on the menu.

Those 93 items were in addition to all the varieties of salsa you could order.

Just after you came to item 93 and past the fresh salsas, the pizza menu began, and there were another dozen of those to choose from.

Back when Jack was having tax issues, which caused him to declare bankruptcy to hold onto his lease, a state auditor sat down with him and demanded to see a list of his creditors, essentially the suppliers he bought his raw materials from.

Jack produced a list. The auditor was shocked to see it had 47 companies on it.

"This is crazy," she said. "No restaurant this small buys from this many people. Why don't you just get everything from one of the two or three major restaurant supply distributors, like everyone else?"

Jack proceeded to tell her each one of his suppliers had one or two things that were better than anything else he could find on the market, so he just bought what he thought were the best ingredients from wherever he could find them. The total simply came to 47.

When Jack could not find a salad dressing supplier that met with his satisfaction, of course he went ahead and made his own, from scratch.

Ninety-three items on his menu, procured from 47 suppliers, and here's Jack in the back of a bankrupt 1200-square-foot restaurant making his own salad dressings.

As if anyone was coming to the Clubhouse Bar-B-Q for the salad dressings.

When I point this out to Jack now, he says, "Well, I guess it does seem a bit eccentric, but at the time it just seemed like the right thing to do."

In any event, it exemplified a passion and an attention to detail that would serve us well.

Jack not only loves to develop food products, but he's astoundingly good at it. It's little wonder, then, that the first batch of Garden Fresh salsa only took Jack 15 minutes to formulate. It is virtually unchanged since, even though it is now replicated more than 800,000 times a year.

I was not there for that first batch of salsa, but I was present for the first batch of Garden Fresh Dips.

Jack and I were in our tiny Garden Fresh test kitchen. (The kitchen was just off our lobby via a tiny hall. That hall was eventually converted into an office for Jack and Annette, who served as Garden Fresh's CEO. They were in there for years.)

Jack thought a cream cheese and salsa dip would connect with our Garden Fresh customer base. He took out a stainless steel mixing bowl and just started adding ingredients, as I wrote down what he was doing. We'd both stick a plastic testing spoon in to try it and, based on our discussion, Jack would tinker with it here and there.

After 20 minutes Jack stopped adding ingredients, said he was happy with it, and so was I. I thought it was terrific. I suggested we let it sit and cure for a day or two to see how it held up.

We did just that, and after a couple days we were even happier but thought that anything could be improved. So over the course of the next month we kept tweaking Jack's initial recipe, which really was not a recipe at all, just his gut feel for what he believed would make a great dip.

I've got a pretty good palate, and Jack has a world-class palate, but every time we'd change something it only served to make the product worse. Nothing we ever did could improve on Jack's initial, instinctual first pitch, so we simply left it as it was, that first day, after 20 minutes of development time.

Over the course of the next couple weeks, whenever we could find the time, we'd meet again in that test kitchen just outside Jack's future hallway office. We proceeded to develop three more varieties: Spinach, Artichoke Spinach & 4 Cheese, and Chipotle—all in the same fashion, all within 20 to 30 minutes, tops, with minimal tinkering afterward. We then launched our new dip line, both at the major account that had initially requested dips as well as at all our other customers.

Today that first flavor we developed, Garden Fresh's Cream Cheese and Salsa Dip, is our best-selling variety.

Strategic Benefit: Garden Fresh grew to eventually become the ninth leading brand of dips in the United States. It's something no other top ten brand of fresh salsa can claim, to have a leading position in this other major deli category, an advantage Garden Fresh can offer that our competitors can't.

COMPETITIVE ADVANTAGE 3: MARGARITAVILLE

I was in New York one day when one of our brokers called me saying he'd heard Jimmy Buffett's Margaritaville Food Group was interested in launching its own line of fresh salsa.

Margaritaville had begun licensing their brand to consumer product companies and had subsequently successfully launched a number of products, including $300 margarita blenders, produced by the multi-billion-dollar consumer products conglomerate Jarden; Margarita mixers, produced by Dr. Pepper/Snapple; and their own line of tequila and beer, produced by Anheuser Busch/InBev.

Intrigued, I called the president of Margaritaville Foods, thinking it would be great to introduce myself and have maybe a five-minute conversation.

It turned out to be a 45-minute conversation. I described our humble origins, how Jack and I had gotten together, our approach to making fresh salsa, as well as our other capabilities.

Two weeks later he flew to Detroit and was at our conference table when he said, "This is the best fresh salsa I've ever had."

It also turned out that he was on the verge of striking a deal with one of our competitors, eight days away, in fact. He called his lawyer to put that deal on hold.

Six months later we closed on a licensing deal with the Margaritaville Food Group. Shortly after that we launched a 17-item Margaritaville deli line.

Strategic Benefit: People have often asked why we'd enter into an arrangement with a brand like Margaritaville, to have this line merchandised next to our own.

I had noticed that virtually none of our customers were offering just Garden Fresh salsa. They'd have our salsa and any number of our competitors in their deli case.

I had also realized that most buyers were trying to rationalize their supplier base. Buyers' work loads had increased so much that the fewer vendor meetings they had to attend the better, and the fewer companies they could transact with, the easier their lives would be. Thus, buying multiple brands from the same supplier was in their best interests.

But brands are tough to build, they just don't happen overnight.

Thus we believed we could offer our buyers our Garden Fresh brand of products, an all natural super premium line that was connecting with consumers on an everyday basis, as well as a second line of deli products, similar but different than our Garden Fresh line, under a national brand that was, frankly, stronger than our own, Margaritaville.

Our buyers would then be able to upgrade their overall deli sets by dropping one of our competitor's inferior lines for our superior Margaritaville line.

By bringing Margaritaville into the Garden Fresh fold, we'd be able to offer something to our buyers that no one else could. We had exclusive rights to the Margaritaville label. None of our competitors could bring this brand to the table, and it dovetailed with what buyers were looking to do anyway—work with fewer vendors. All while improving the quality of what they were selling to their consumers.

But getting the Margaritaville line off the ground was easier said than done, particularly with respect to one aspect of the line.

After the president of Margaritaville Foods contacted his lawyer to put his previous deal on hold, I invited him to lunch. On our way to the restaurant I told him I did not just want to be his fresh salsa manufacturer—that I wanted to be able to offer our buyers an entire deli line of Margaritaville branded items, including tortilla chips.

"Oh," he responded. "We've already looked at the tortilla chip category and have decided we don't want to have Margaritaville represented there."

After lunch I took him to the nearest Kroger, which just happened to be in one of the wealthiest enclaves in metro Detroit. The store is beautiful. We proceeded to the deli section so he could see how Garden Fresh is merchandised, in general, and more specifically how all our lines work in concert with each other to truly make a presence at store level—a classic "rising tides lifts all boats" strategy.

I'm literally on my home turf here so you'd think we'd plan these things in advance, but in truth we're not that clever; unbeknownst to me Kroger was having a sale on our Garden Fresh line and throughout the deli were four enormous displays of our chips.

Our chip bags are bright orange and the entire department seemed to be glowing like the sun. They were everywhere, just these massive walls of brilliant color screaming "Garden Fresh." You couldn't turn around without seeing more of them.

As soon as we got out of the store and into the parking lot, the president of Margaritaville Foods said, "I see what you mean—you guys can have chips too."

There was just one problem; we did not have any place to make them.

―――――

COMPETITIVE ADVANTAGE 4: TORTILLA CHIPS

For a couple of years after Jack made that first batch of fresh salsa in that five-gallon bucket, he would deliver the product himself, eventually handling 70 accounts. Before he could afford a truck, he simply used his car.

No matter that Garden Fresh Salsa is a fresh product that needs to be refrigerated. "Back then I considered air conditioning 'refrigeration,'" Jack now says.

One day Jack made a delivery to a single store in Detroit's historic Eastern Market. The proprietor said, "You know, people love chips with their salsa. You should come out with some tortilla chips to go with this."

Jack thought it was a great idea and set out to develop a line of Garden Fresh Gourmet tortilla chips.

Rather than look for an established tortilla chip manufacturer, however, who might be able to professionally produce a line under the

Garden Fresh label, he took the bootstrapping entrepreneur approach, consistent with how Jack started Garden Fresh salsa.

So Jack retreated to the back of his 1200-square-foot restaurant. He would order fresh tortillas, cut them by hand, then drop them into his French fry fryer. When they reached the golden brown color he was looking for, he pulled them out, salted them, put them in a cellophane bag, hand-applied a label, and sealed the bag with a twist-tie.

Two years and 135,000 bags later, and "more cuts and burns on my hands than I care to remember, let's just say they were everywhere," Jack moved his chip operation into the formerly abandoned video store where Garden Fresh Salsa was also now being made.

Before long, Jack was up to eight French fry fryers, lining the back of the video store. There'd be two operators, each handling four fryers, making chips in two-pound batches. When the chips were ready they'd pull the baskets out of the oil, turn around, and dump them onto a stainless steel bin, where they'd be salted.

The bin had four holes in it, and an employee would scoop the chips into the hole into a bag below, weigh the bag, and then add or subtract chips to get to the proper net weight.

The only problem was you can't put hot chips in a bag, as condensation soon occurs and the chips wilt in the bag. So Jack instructed his new manager overseeing chips, Tom Schliep, to go to Home Depot and buy some fans.

"Some" fans soon turned into eight fans. Tom rigged them all to be just a couple feet above the stainless steel bin, to cool the chips prior to them being filled.

"We referred to it as 'fan world,'" Tom recalls. "There were cords everywhere."

One problem they could not solve was the oil. When the fryer operator would pull the basket out of the oil, turn, and dump the chips into the bin, oil would invariably drip onto the floor.

"There was oil all over the place, including the cords," Tom says. "People was constantly slipping and falling."

The oil would also seep into Tom's clothes; at the time he was driving a car with cloth seats. One time Jack got into the car with him.

"What's this smell?" Jack asked, only to be told it was rancid frying oil that had been transferred from Tom's clothes to his seats.

This process went on for years, and as Garden Fresh's chip business grew Tom realized it was unsustainable so he started looking for other solutions. He found a small tortilla manufacturer in southwest Detroit who agreed to run chips through their fryer.

So for the next year Tom would get to the Garden Fresh chip plant at 3:30 a.m., load four pallets of uncooked chips on his truck, run them down to the plant in southwest Detroit, and have them run through their fryer. He'd then load the bulk chips back onto his truck and take them back to Garden Fresh's chip and salsa plant, where Garden Fresh employees were waiting to bag them.

As Garden Fresh's chip business grew, our chip supplier was able to set up their own tortilla chip line, and after a while full production was transferred to their plant.

Shortly after I became a partner at Garden Fresh, Jack took me to the chip plant to show me the operation. . . let's just say no one was confusing this plant with one of those sterile computer chip deals you see on TV.

Our supplier had set up their line in what amounted to an alley with a roof over it, with chain link gates on either side that served as doors. As I was standing there, I thought: "This is currently Garden Fresh's best-selling item, our Original Tortilla Chips."

Over time we gradually got them to improve their operations, and to this day they're a terrific partner of ours. However, it soon became clear to me that they would not be able to meet Garden Fresh's long-term needs, so I began to look for an alternative.

I found a firm in Grand Rapids, Michigan, The El Matador Tortilla Chip Company, that was making chips in the authentic, Hispanic fashion, using real corn and grinding it into a mash using volcanic stones. Virtually no one makes chips like this anymore.

Most tortilla chips produced in the United States are made with corn flour that is hydrated, stamped into a chip, and run through a fryer. The end result is a chip of cardboard-like consistency, which most companies find acceptable, as to them the chip is merely a delivery vehicle for their spices, which is where tortilla chip manufacturers devote most of their efforts.

Think of Doritos; that snack is defined by the spices, not the chip. Frito-Lay completely saturates the product with their flavorings; the actual chip is an afterthought.

But truly great tortilla chips are made with real corn. Most companies that do use real corn don't use volcanic stones to grind the corn into a mash, as the stones have to be re-filed virtually after every shift. Instead, they use stainless steel wheels that never have to be touched.

But if you truly want an authentic, Hispanic tortilla chip, you have to use real corn, not flour, and you have to grind the corn into a mash using volcanic stones, not stainless steel wheels. Employing this method is the only way you'll get great consistency, including flavor blisters, which will provide the most powerful flavor profile.

Of course, anything less would not be sufficient for Garden Fresh. That would not be consistent with our brand promise: to be the best product on the market.

If we could not produce a genuine, top-of-the-market chip, we'd rather not be in the category. And despite whatever shortcomings our current supplier might possess, their chip was authentic. They used real corn ground into a mash with volcanic stones.

So when I first walked into El Matador and learned that they made chips in this same fashion, which very few people do anymore, I couldn't believe my luck.

My luck soon ran out, though, when I was introduced to the owner, Mike Navarro.

Mr. Navarro was a Mexican immigrant who had somehow ended up in mid-Michigan; in 1980 he founded his own tortilla chip company. By the time I met him, he was in his late seventies. While his El Matador Tortilla Chip was wildly popular in the Grand Rapids environs, he never grew his business much beyond that and was doing maybe $1.5 million per year.

I soon found out why. Let's just say Mr. Navarro was a challenging person to be associated with.

He felt completely comfortable calling me his "gringo." He told me he had turned down a multi-million-dollar private label chip opportunity with one of the largest retailers in Michigan because the buyer called him when he was gardening: "I didn't appreciate that and I told him so."

Then he not so delicately told me his response to that buyer also included an F-bomb. This was a man who was either incredibly passionate about his gardening or really was not interested in growing his business.

Assuming the latter, I figured he had no desire to produce Garden Fresh's chips, which he confirmed on the spot: "You're damn right, gringo."

I then asked if he'd be interested in selling El Matador, and he had me call his accountant, a terrific guy based in South Bend, Indiana. He and I instantly hit it off, but he told me right from the get-go that I was wasting my time. Mr. Navarro would never sell.

He said that the tiny El Matador Tortilla Chip Company was Mr. Navarro's life's work, and more importantly, it had become his identity, that it represented his social standing in his community. This was not about money. It was about what money could not buy.

I took him at his word. Over the years we stayed in touch. I'd call him every few months, but nothing ever changed with Mr. Navarro, and we found ourselves talking about Notre Dame football as much as anything else.

All the while I was simultaneously trying to buy or at least partner with our current chip supplier, but they absolutely wanted to remain independent.

For years I'd try to get the husband and wife team to either let us invest in their company, to help them get to the size required to meet our growing needs, or to let us buy them outright. I eventually started working with their accountant and their lawyer, both of whom advised them to partner with us in some respect, but the owners just could not bring themselves to do so.

Finally, their lawyer, who was also their financial advisor, told me they were simply people who would rather own 100 percent of something relatively small than 20 percent of something huge, even if that was not in their best financial interests.

I completely understood. If there was anything I had learned about being a business owner it was that, as arduous as it might be, you do get used to being your own boss real fast, and it's not a lifestyle you readily give up.

So when the president of Margaritaville Foods uttered those fateful words to me in the parking lot of that upscale Kroger in suburban Detroit: "OK, I get it, you've got tortilla chips too," I knew I needed to do something. Our current supplier could not make all the Garden Fresh chips we were selling, let alone handle Margaritaville as well.

I called El Matador's accountant in South Bend one last time and told him we were more motivated than ever. He said our timing was impeccable; Mr. Navarro's wife had been diagnosed with emphysema and had been given 12 months to live, and that their children wanted to get their money out of the company.

Their accountant convinced Mrs. Navarro that something had to be done and that this was the time to do it. No one would pay more than Garden Fresh or close more quickly, and if she and Mr. Navarro wanted to take care of their children's financial needs after they were gone, now was the time to act.

It wasn't an easy deal to close, as Mr. Navarro proved challenging right until the end.

I brought Jack and Annette to Grand Rapids to meet with Mr. Navarro. We endured a four-hour soliloquy on topics ranging from the Spanish Inquisition to immigration reform. Just continuous, stream-of-conscious rambling—he never seemed to pause to breathe. It was literally impossible to jump in and contribute to the conversation. We just sat there and listened. Incessantly.

Jack was also a fellow "gringo," and Mr. Navarro was still quite adept at dropping F-bombs, which his wife would wince at repeatedly. At one point she even reminded him that women were present at the table, but there was no stopping Mr. Navarro.

We had to promise him that we'd keep a portrait of him and his wife in the lobby. That he could keep his hand-carved doors leading into his conference room. That his friends could still meet every day in the front lobby for their 3:00 p.m. "Knights of the Roundtable" card-playing session. And that his children would be employed with the company moving forward.

Mr. Navarro called the day we closed the worst day of his life, and he never set foot in the El Matador plant again.

But close we did, a mere two weeks before we closed on our licensing deal with Margaritaville Foods, which included the rights to produce tortilla chips under that brand.

Finally, we had a plant in which to produce them. . . as if there were ever a doubt.

Strategic Benefit: Garden Fresh is the only top ten brand of fresh salsa that also makes its own tortilla chips. On the surface the benefits are two-fold, but deep down they're beyond quantifiable.

If you think about a pint of fresh salsa, there's not much real estate on the container in which to declare who you are and what makes you special. But contrast that small 16-ounce container to a tortilla chip bag, one that will stand behind your pint of salsa in a deli case; the land mass is immense. It results in a veritable billboard effect for your brand.

In one of our Garden Fresh PowerPoint presentations we have a photograph, taken directly from a major national retailer, of a full cooler display housing both our Garden Fresh deli line as well as our competitor's. Above the Garden Fresh line, on the top of the back wall of the cooler, are rows of our shockingly orange Garden Fresh Tortilla Chips, tremendously elevating our brand presence.

Above our competitor's line is someone else's brand of cored pineapple.

Which brand would you rather own?

In addition, the cross-merchandising opportunities are incredible. Nothing complements salsa more than tortilla chips. In fact, tortilla chips are the primary delivery vehicle for salsa.

Thus, Garden Fresh's line of tortilla chips is a tremendous strategic advantage for us—to be the only brand of fresh salsa in the display case with rows of large Garden Fresh branded tortilla chips bags positioned directly behind them. Then to be able to cross-promote them, such as by buying two pints of salsa and receiving a free bag of chips. That's simply something no other company in our field can offer.

COMPETITIVE ADVANTAGE 5: HUMMUS

You hear of deals being made on the golf course, but never on the George Washington bridge in New York City. But that's exactly where the genesis of the Garden Fresh Hummus division took place.

I was trying to persuade Jack to make hummus, as this was a market I was convinced we needed to be in.

As previously mentioned, Jack's not the type of guy you have to ask twice to develop a new product. That's the good news. The bad news is that hummus is not an easy product to make, and try as Jack did, for months, nothing we came up with was worthy of the Garden Fresh brand.

We just couldn't satisfy our brand promise to be the best, primarily due to one competitor.

There was a company in New York, just a few minutes from LaGuardia Airport, that was making hummus like no other company in this country. It was called Sabra Dipping Company.

Sabra was the company that brought the ancient Mediterranean style of making hummus employing dried chickpeas, instead of canned, to this country. The result was a superior, creamy hummus unlike anything else in America.

Sabra had clearly created a breakthrough product. Frankly, they had done for hummus what Garden Fresh had done for fresh salsa—taken their category to a new level.

Jack had befriended the president of Sabra at a food show, and soon Jack and I were traveling to New York to see whether they'd be interested in private labeling a line of hummus for us. In turn, we offered to private label our salsa for them.

Talks between Garden Fresh and Sabra were progressing until Sabra made the strategic decision that salsa, which is a product of Hispanic origins, would not be appropriate for their brand, which was Mediterranean in nature.

I couldn't argue with that logic.

And furthermore, I was told, Sabra wanted to strictly focus on hummus, believing it was better to be deep in one category than broad in many.

Nothing wrong with that either, though it differed from Garden Fresh's strategy to enter other categories to best meet our deli buyers' needs.

Then Sabra entered into a contract to purchase the leading brand of hummus in the metro Detroit market, Garden Fresh's home turf, a company called Basha.

At that time Basha was the largest brand in the Detroit market. In addition, Basha possessed a larger share of their top-25 market than any other hummus in the United States. Although Basha used canned chickpeas, it was clearly a bold move by Sabra to gain considerable market share—right in our own backyard.

The Sabra deal to buy Basha dragged on for months. In the interim, not only was Jack still struggling to figure out how to make hummus but the president of Sabra, whom we befriended, had been unceremoniously fired and was soon running a label company in New Jersey—ironically the company that made Sabra's labels.

Which brings us back to me crossing the George Washington Bridge and the birth of the Garden Fresh hummus division.

I flew into New York to meet with this label company, at the former president of Sabra/new president of this label company's request, and he picked me up at the airport.

As we were crossing the George Washington Bridge I asked him if he thought Sabra was ever going to close on Basha. Since Sabra had decided not to make hummus for us, I wanted to buy Basha and use that as our entrée into the hummus market.

He told me that one of the leading hummus manufacturers in Israel, a company called Strauss, was about to purchase a majority interest in Sabra and that Strauss had no interest in this little hummus company in Detroit.

Thus, the Basha deal would never close.

The next evening, back in Detroit, I had dinner with the owner of Basha and told him what I had learned in New York: that Sabra would never buy Basha.

I also offered to buy Basha on the spot, for the exact terms that Sabra had agreed to pay.

We closed on Basha two months later, and sure enough we were in the hummus business.

That former president of Sabra, who left to run Sabra's label company? We subsequently hired him to be our chief operating officer. Let's just say he was bitter, which can be a good thing, we learned.

Soon he and Jack were on their way to Israel and came back with $1.9 million of equipment so that we could make Garden Fresh hummus the authentic, Mediterranean way, using dried chickpeas, not canned, that were roasted, whipped into a mash, and cured overnight in a blast chiller on cookie sheets.

Thus, the same man who set up Sabra's breakthrough hummus concept was setting up ours.

I still refer to this as Jack's finest hour with respect to the Garden Fresh line.

Basha was a terrific hummus, and its market share in the southeastern Michigan region was extraordinary. But that was not good enough for Garden Fresh; if it was not the absolute best on the market, it was not worthy of the Garden Fresh brand. So Jack was off to Israel with the guy who had set up Sabra's hummus operations, because if you want to have authentic, Mediterranean hummus you've got to make it the right way—no cutting corners.

Strategic Benefit: Garden Fresh eventually grew to become the third largest hummus manufacturer in the United States, something no other top ten brand of fresh salsa can say. In addition, we are one of the few who produce hummus employing authentic, old-world Mediterranean methods. In a world in which buyers are trying to rationalize their vendor base, to be able to get a world class line of hummus from the same company they can get the number 1 national brand of fresh salsa from makes their lives much easier and gives them a reason to naturally gravitate toward us.

While Jack was in Israel with Sabra's former president/our new chief operating officer, I received a call from the buyer at one of Basha's largest accounts.

He was incensed. The Basha all natural hummus we were selling him was fermenting, bloating after only a week on the shelf, whereas under the old regime he was getting a 30-day shelf life.

"This is so typical. A big company takes over a smaller line and there goes the quality. I've seen this movie a thousand times before."

I assured him that was not our style and that I'd get back to him with an answer.

I checked with our operations guys and they assured me they had not changed a thing, that they were following the Basha all natural recipe exactly.

So I called the now former owner of Basha and asked him for help, as we just could not figure out what we were doing wrong.

"Oh, that's easy," he told me. "You just have to add some sodium benzoate and potassium sorbate to the recipe."

I told him he had misunderstood me. . . that those were preservatives that we added to the regular Basha line but that I was inquiring as to what he did for the Basha all natural line.

"No, I heard you the first time. How do you think we got a 30-day shelf life? Without preservatives you're only going to get five to seven days."

That explained a lot. Now I understood why our Basha all natural line was bloating. We proceeded to drop that account, as at the time we could not produce an all natural line of hummus, not honestly anyway.

The ability to do that would come shortly thereafter, thanks to a radical new technology called high pressure pasteurization (HPP).

————

COMPETITIVE ADVANTAGE 6: HIGH PRESSURE PASTEURIZATION (HPP)

It was the summer of 2008, and Jack had finally had enough.

"$700 to repaint her kitchen? That's it—we're getting that HPP machine."

If only it had been just $700.

High *pressure* pasteurization (HPP) was a technique developed in Japan in the late 1980s and pioneered in this country about a decade later by a Seattle-based company called Avure.

It's a revolutionary way to pasteurize food.

The conventional method to pasteurize food is to heat it to 180 degrees and hold it at that temperature for ten seconds.

You're essentially cooking the food.

When you cook food you kill the food-borne pathogens such as mold, yeast, and bacteria. Unfortunately, you also kill much of the flavor profile.

With HPP you never cook the food.

You subject the product to tremendous pressure — 80,000 pounds per square inch, or five times the pressure found anywhere in nature, which is at the bottom of the ocean. And you're doing this in 43-degree water, so the flavor profile is maintained.

HPP technology made the fresh guacamole you're now enjoying in your deli department possible. Without it, guacamole could only be made available in a frozen state. In fact, the fresh guacamole manufacturers were first to embrace HPP.

Today HPP is becoming more prevalent. Lunch meat companies are employing it in some of their items, as they don't have to use fillers or nitrates to preserve their products; in addition, they taste better and have a longer shelf life.

And the fresh juice craze is largely being fueled by HPP. Pasteurizing juice by heating it to 180 degrees severely degrades the flavor profile. Pasteurizing it by subjecting it to pressure in 43-degree water maintains the flavor profile. Starbucks bought a company called Evolution in 2011 and recently opened a $70 million HPP plant in California.

But that is now. In 2008 most of our buyers could only spell HPP; they really had no idea what it was about or what it could do.

Jack was one of the true visionaries, particularly in the deli space, with respect to the potential of this new technology.

In fact, one of the first meetings I ever had with Jack was five years earlier, in 2003, with a major Midwest distributor, Spartan Foods in Grand Rapids, Michigan.

We were in our buyer's office and Jack was telling him about this breakthrough technology that had burst onto the food scene and that we were soon going to purchase *two* HPP machines.

HPP machines are $2 million each. I remember walking out into the parking lot after the meeting and saying to Jack: "We're a $4 million company. We can't afford one $2 million HPP machine, let alone two."

But Jack was determined, even obsessed—to his credit—with what this technology could do for Garden Fresh. We just had to grow to a point at which we could afford it, and have a very compelling reason to finally pull the trigger.

Well, it took us five years to grow to the point at which we could afford an HPP machine, and even then we needed some financial gymnastics to make that happen. The $700 check we cut to a customer in Canada proved to be that compelling reason.

A couple years earlier, Costco had picked up Garden Fresh Salsa. It wasn't long before Costco became our largest customer.

But we were soon facing a major, existential problem.

Food companies want their products to "explode off the shelves." That's a slang expression meaning your product is selling extremely well, which is a good thing. Our salsa, though, was literally exploding *on* the shelves, which is never a good thing.

Because our salsa is fresh and never cooked, if our product ever gets above 40 degrees the fresh vegetables we use ferment. The fermentation process produces a gas that, in an air-tight container, causes the package to expand, or bloat, as there is simply no place for the gas to escape. When this happens, our salsa packages look like footballs on the shelf. The product is actually still safe to eat, although it's acidic with respect to flavor profile, but the product looks spoiled. It's clearly unsalable.

We had always struggled with fermentation in our conventional retailer 16-ounce package, but had largely been able to contain it.

Costco is not a conventional retailer. They employ the club format, which demands larger volumes, and in the fresh salsa category that typically means packaging your product in a container three times the 16-ounce size, or 48 ounces.

In our 48-ounce club format size, we just could not control the fermentation, possibly due to the exponential effect of having triple the amount of fresh vegetables in a single container.

Our product was bloating all over Costco's North American shelves, often to the point where lids were popping off the containers—literally exploding **on** the shelves.

I was on the phone with Costco's quality assurance director virtually every day. I could tell we were about to be pulled from our largest account if we did not solve this problem.

Then we received a call, followed by e-mailed pictures, from a woman in Canada. Her pictures depicted salsa all over the ceiling in her kitchen, after a 48-ounce container of our Garden Fresh Salsa had exploded when placed on her counter.

Jack felt like we had no other choice but to finally purchase that HPP machine he had been dreaming about for years.

So we cut the woman in Canada a check for $700 so that she could re-paint her kitchen ceiling and ordered our first HPP machine for $1.96 million.

Avure was making their HPP machines in Sweden. Each one weighs 105,000 pounds and we had to get a police escort to take it through the state of Ohio. When it finally arrived, two cranes were required just to take if off the truck.

It was like they were bringing in the Space Shuttle.

On top of the $1.96 million cost for the HPP machine, we had to spend another $400,000 just to equip our facility. We had to rip up the floor in our plant and put in an additional six feet of concrete to support it. We then spent $135000 to upgrade our electrical capacity.

And then there was the learning curve.

HPP machines are not things you just plug in, flip a switch, and get going with. We proceeded to spend another $600,000 trying to figure out how to use high pressure pasteurization in the deli space, something no one was doing at the time.

Jack kept calling the machine's manufacturer, Avure, for technical assistance until it got to the point where they were telling him: "You're on your own here; no one is even trying to do what you're doing. In fact, tell us when you figure it out. We're curious ourselves."

The only part of this equation we could really afford was the $700 check we cut to that poor woman in Canada. We certainly did not have the other $3 million or so lying around to get our HPP program off the ground.

And $3 million is not exactly an amount you can secure via a Discover credit card loan. We were way past that.

Then our accountant came up with a plan. We could apply for a $7 million Industrial Revenue Bond on the tortilla chip company, El Matador, that we had just purchased for roughly $4 million, then use the excess proceeds, $3 million, to purchase the HPP machine. What our lenders did not know would not hurt them.

Somehow the bond was approved.

It turned out to be the most improbable financing scenario imaginable. We had scrambled to buy a tortilla chip plant so that we could live up to our previously made commitment to produce chips for Margaritaville, a commitment we made before we had a plant to make them in. That deal then became the source of capital that we hoped would allow us to keep what had become our largest customer.

Jack told me to be in our lawyer's office at 1:00 p.m. on Tuesday of the following week for the bond closing. I told him that would be tight for me as I had a plane to catch shortly thereafter for a sales meeting.

"Oh, don't worry, this won't take long."

When I walked into our attorney's offices, I was instructed to go into their main conference room, which housed what is to this day the largest table I've ever seen, which was convenient, as on that conference table there were 43 separate stacks of papers that we had to sign to secure an Industrial Revenue Bond. Each stack was easily six inches high—just am amazing amount of paper.

Before long the lawyers were just opening all the stacks to the signature pages so I could sign them before I rushed out the door to catch my plane—which I made, by the way. To this day I have no idea what I signed. I do know the payments on the bond were $58,000 per month, though.

I also know that our fermentation issues at Costco stopped, dead in their tracks, once we started HPP-ing our 48-ounce club format salsa. It was like turning on a light switch, going from total darkness to complete enlightenment. Zero issues, throughout North America.

Strategic Benefit: No one in the deli space does more with HPP than Garden Fresh. In fact, Garden Fresh has been one of the true pioneers in this area and has developed a level of expertise none of our competitors can match. In addition, there are products that can only be made available with HPP technology; thus, Garden Fresh can offer our customers unique items that no one else can.

Avure, the Seattle-based HPP machine manufacturer, took notice that Garden Fresh was doing things in the deli space that no one else was even attempting, so they invited Jack and me to a conference they were hosting at their HPP assembly plant in Sweden.

At that conference I made a presentation on all we were doing with HPP technology; there were attendees from four continents and 16 countries. Jack answered questions from the audience afterward.

En route back to Detroit from Stockholm, we had a layover in Amsterdam. Once we were on board, the pilot announced that we'd be delayed due to our flight plan being re-routed over Italy to compensate for the ash being generated by a volcano in Greenland.

Fifteen minutes later the pilot said that we'd be delayed again, as the ash was getting worse and they were going to have to re-route our flight over Germany.

A few minutes after that, he said it appeared that every airport in Europe was going to be shut down for five days due to the ash.

Jack and I looked at each other and I suggested that, if we were to be stranded in Europe for five days, we should take a train to Paris, my favorite city anywhere, and bide our time there.

"Oh perfect. I can just imagine trying to explain to my wife why I'm spending five days in Paris with you. Who gets stranded in Europe by a volcano? She'll never believe me."

The pilot came back on and told us that, if we could pull away from the gate in 10 minutes, we were cleared for takeoff, and that we'd literally be one of the last planes to leave European airspace for five days.

I've never seen 350 people move so fast, but our boondoggle to Paris was off.

HPP was working like a charm, exceeding our expectations, and our business at our largest account had been saved. Jack's long-held vision had been realized.

What we didn't realize, though, was that HPP would not only save our business at our largest account. It would also enable us to catch and ride the biggest wave in U.S. food retailing in decades, the private label phenomenon.

———

COMPETITIVE ADVANTAGE 7: PRIVATE LABEL

I was at a vendor conference with one of the largest conventional food retailer in the United States. Their president was addressing the audience: "We have Kellogg's Corn Flakes and they have Kellogg's Corn Flakes. We have Pampers diapers and they have Pampers diapers. The difference is they're both cheaper there, and they always will be."

The "they" he was referring to was Wal-Mart.

Wal-Mart, of course, was founded by Sam Walton in 1962.

In 1987 they made the fateful decision to start selling food, and the following year opened their first Wal-Mart Supercenter.

In that relatively short period of time, Wal-Mart has secured just under 30 percent of the U.S. food market. It's nothing short of a remarkable achievement, and it has posed an incredible challenge to their competitors.

So if you're the president of a Wal-Mart competitor, you've got a problem: you're never going to compete with your largest competitor on price. Your prices are always going to be higher than theirs.

So what do you do? The president outlined a two-pronged approach.

First, he said, they needed to beat Wal-Mart on selection, particularly around the perimeter of the store, meaning in the deli, bakery, produce, meat, and seafood sections. He believed his company could offer better variety and higher quality products in those areas than Wal-Mart could. That was paramount, as he was conceding the center of the store, the grocery section, to Wal-Mart with respect to price.

The second thing he was focused on was developing products under brands that could only be found on his shelves, not ever on Wal-Mart's shelves, proprietary to his company only.

These products are referred to as "private label."

The goal is to have customers fall in love with the private-label brands to the extent that they'll be willing to drive past Wal-Mart to shop at supermarkets chains that have the brands that can only be bought there.

Thus, even though other chains and Wal-Mart still have both Kellogg's Corn Flakes and Pampers, with Wal-Mart still selling at lower prices, private labels offer retailers brands that are exclusive to them. Wal-Mart will not ever be able to offer these products, let alone at a lower price.

Virtually every major retailer in the United States is adopting this same strategy, something that European retailers have been doing for years.

Most major food manufacturers, however, opt not to produce private label products for retailers, preferring instead to create value with their own brands. They would prefer not to have retailers benefit from their product development expertise and have private label programs undercut their own national brands on price.

It's a challenging and vexing strategic decision for every food manufacturer. As it was for Garden Fresh, too.

Do we go all in and support our own brands, and keep our break-through flavor profiles, the result of our almost unheard of artisanal approach to manufacturing, to ourselves? Or do we agree to make all this expertise available to our retail customers in the form of their own private label brands, which would in essence often be merchandised right next to our own products—and at a lower price?

We decided to be true not only to our commitment to make best-in-class products, but to also be true to our commitment to be true strategic partners with our retail customers. To not simply develop transactional relationships with them but to recognize their legitimate needs and concerns and to work with them in concert with their business models.

Thus, we made the strategic decision to private label our products for our retail customers, something most of our major competitors don't do.

As a result it is not unusual to walk into a major retailer and see Garden Fresh Salsa merchandised in the deli cooler and a retailer's private label salsa sitting right next to our line—with both brands coming out of our plant.

While our decision to engage in private label programs is controversial, we've noticed that our partnerships with our retail customers are invariable strengthened and that our own Garden Fresh brand is strengthened as well.

There's a certain alchemy, magic almost, that occurs when you're producing a retailer's private label products, especially when you're recognized as the premier manufacturer in your field. They're going to carry their own brand and at least one national brand. It sure does make their world a lot easier if they can deal with one company for both of those needs.

A couple years after attending that conference, I attended another conference with Kroger.

Kroger had recently launched a line of private label salsa with another vendor, and it was not selling very well.

I introduced myself to the Kroger executive in charge of that particular program and offered to help.

A week later I was back in Cincinnati meeting with her and her boss. Once they saw all Garden Fresh could do, including our HPP expertise, they began working with us to take over this program.

We did so, in record time, and were named the Kroger Perishable Vendor of the year.

Strategic Benefit: Most of our major competitors won't produce private labels for retailers, even though it is the fastest growing segment of the U.S. food industry. Garden Fresh, however, recognizes how important private label programs are, strategically, to our customers, national retailers; thus we choose to provide this service.

JUST SHOW UP

After all this, when I sit down with a buyer I can represent capabilities that no one else he or she will ever meet with can.

I and only I can claim that I can offer the number 1 brand of fresh salsa in the United States. I'm the only top ten brand of salsa that also can offer a top ten line of dips. The same is true for tortilla chips. I have exclusive rights to the Margaritaville label. We're a top five line of hummus. We not only have new world technology like high pressure pasteurization, but we're doing more with it than anyone else in our industry. We are, unlike our major competitors, willing to private label for our major accounts.

After all that, if we can't grow that buyer's business in some fashion, something is wrong. Either the buyer is brain dead or is about to retire and stopped caring a while ago.

I don't "sell" anything in my meetings with buyers. I merely have conversations in which I list what we can bring to the table, capabilities that, due to the approach we took to building Garden Fresh, I know none of our competitors can match.

I listen to what a buyer's particular needs might be. I know that I have more arrows in my quiver to meet whatever those needs are than anyone else he could ever meet with.

The same is true for the balance of our sales force.

To paraphrase Woody Allen; to be successful, then, when our sales force shows up, they're 80 percent of the way there.

Secret 5: Would Woody Be Proud of Your Company?

How can you build a company that Woody Allen would be proud of?

The key is not to just develop *products or services,* but instead to develop *strategic advantages*—advantages that your competitors can't possibly match.

For just as no one is interested in "me too" products, no one is interested in "me too" companies.

Building such a company requires you not to operate simply from the ground level, but to strategically plan from the 15,000-foot level. Where you can see over the trees. Where you can hover above your customers' complete set of needs.

From this lofty perch you can take a holistic approach to developing your company, one in which you're offering a range of capabilities that your customers can purchase from you and only you.

One in which your sales force only has to show up to be successful.

And when they do show up, all they have to do is listen to their customers' needs and they'll have the tools available to meet them.

That's their job. Yours is to ensure they have more tools in their toolbox than anyone else.

6

Value Values

Your beliefs become your thoughts,
Your thoughts become your words,
Your words become your actions,
Your actions become your habits,
Your habits become your values,
Your values become your destiny.

—Mahatma Gandhi

So many people believe that business is about compromising your values.

Compromising your product in order to hit financial margins.

Compromising your employees for profit.

Doing whatever is necessary to make the sale, whether it is in your customer's interests or not.

Giving back to your community only when it is in your company's best interests to do so.

Adhering to your core, human values, however, can actually put you at an advantage, an advantage that over time will help you create more value than you ever will by compromising them for short-term gains, for apparent business reasons.

Over the course of my first decade at Garden Fresh, we faced several significant challenges, often existential in nature.

The core, human values that we held dear throughout these events in the end truly shaped our destiny.

And created tremendous value.

———

RESOLVE

Just after I became a partner at Garden Fresh, a competing brand of fresh salsa, also emanating from metro Detroit, was launched: Chuck & Dave's.

It rocked Jack and Annette to their very core.

I had never met either Chuck or Dave, but Chuck was Garden Fresh's former operations manager and Dave had been Garden Fresh's production and maintenance supervisor.

So integral to Garden Fresh operations were they that Jack and Annette had promised them 10 percent of the company if they stayed for three years.

But rather than honor that agreement, Chuck and Dave decided to bolt Garden Fresh and set up their own plant about 20 minutes away.

They were incredibly brazen in their actions.

They incorporated their holding company, Buddies Foods, while they were still employed by Garden Fresh.

They signed a lease for their plant while they were still employed by Garden Fresh.

They approached two of Garden Fresh's customers, both of whom had reasons to want a competing salsa manufacturer in their market, which Chuck and Dave were aware of due to their intimate knowledge of Garden Fresh's business, and convinced both of them to let Buddies Foods make salsa for them.

They launched eight varieties of fresh salsa that were virtually indistinguishable from Garden Fresh's.

Where Garden Fresh had an "Artichoke Garlic" variety, Chuck and Dave had an "Artichoke & Garlic."

Where Garden Fresh had a "Mango Peach" variety, Chuck and Dave had a "Peach Mango."

Where Garden Fresh had a "Vidalia Onion" variety, Chuck and Dave had a "Sweet Onion."

Sometimes they did not even bother to distinguish themselves. Garden Fresh had a "Thick & Chunky" variety, and Chuck and Dave had a "Thick & Chunky" variety, too.

The ingredients employed in Garden Fresh Salsa and Buddies Salsa were virtually indistinguishable, too. The only difference was that Chuck and Dave added preservatives to their salsa, whereas Garden Fresh was all natural and preservative-free.

Other than that, they were the exact same products, made by two of the few people who had access to Jack's Garden Fresh Salsa recipes—made by two of Jack and Annette's now former employees.

Jack said he lost six pounds the day he heard what his two former partners had done. The pit in his stomach was that profound.

Annette said she barely slept for the next two years.

"We had just built that brand new 25,000-square-foot plant," Jack told me. "And we had borrowed $1.6 million to do so. And here were two of our most trusted employees running lean and mean in a smaller facility, and they had already stolen two of our biggest customers."

For Chuck and Dave it was pure greed and simple math. At the time they were setting up Buddies Foods, Garden Fresh was about a $4 million business, thus their 10 percent stake was worth maybe $400,000.

By poaching two of Garden Fresh's largest customers, however, Buddies Foods was an instant $1.5 million business, and they figured they'd rather own 100 percent of that.

What I'm not sure they did figure on, though, was that Garden Fresh would pursue them relentlessly in the courts.

After 18 months of seemingly endless depositions and legal maneuvers, not to mention $250,000 in legal fees for Garden Fresh alone, *Garden Fresh Gourmet v. Buddies Foods* finally went to trial before a jury in suburban Detroit.

On the morning of the first day of the trial, Jack and I were having breakfast together alone in the courthouse cafeteria. In walked Chuck and Dave with their attorney. Until then I had never even been in the same room with them.

Jack was as nervous and shook up as I've ever seen him, either before or since. Like me, he's a lover and not a fighter, and he was dreading every moment of this pending trial.

Out of nowhere he suddenly blurts out: "I want you to go over there and offer Chuck and Dave $400,000 for Buddies Foods, right now, and this will be over."

I was stunned. Not only did I think Buddies would have been a lousy strategic fit of us, but that company was the last thing I wanted to own. In addition, it would have broken my heart to see Chuck and Dave profit from what they had done to Jack and Annette and Garden Fresh.

Fortunately, I was able to talk Jack out of it and the trial began.

It lasted a full week. Both Jack and I testified. Jack said doing so "was easy for me because all I had to do was tell the truth."

Chuck and Dave's defense was a folly, at best; the records were clear regarding when they incorporated their company and when they signed their lease, all of which occurred while at least one of them was still working for Garden Fresh.

As for the recipes they were employing to make salsa that tasted shockingly like Garden Fresh Salsa, where they not only used to work but had access to those recipes?

They said they found them on the Internet.

After five long days, the trial ended and the jury was charged with rendering a verdict.

It did not take them long to do so; they found Buddies Foods guilty on all counts and made them pay Garden Fresh $660,000 in restitution. The judge furthermore insisted they change their salsa recipes.

It was an exhilarating moment for Garden Fresh.

But we soon learned that, unlike the movies, where a verdict is rendered in your favor and everyone hugs each other and it's over, being awarded a verdict and collecting it are two different experiences.

Chuck and Dave proceeded to declare bankruptcy. Thus those $250,000 in legal fees we had already expended grew to $325,000 in legal fees as we chased Buddies Foods through bankruptcy court while they tried to negotiate the settlement with us.

We never capitulated. In the end Buddies Foods did pay Garden Fresh all they owed over the course of the next seven years.

Looking back, Jack says it was the best thing that ever happened to him, "because I did not have to be partners with Chuck and Dave. Thank God for that."

But the Chuck and Dave's affair affected him profoundly in another fashion as well.

Jack came out of the trial a different person than when he went in. He was much more confident, much more assured of himself.

And deservedly so. He had been tested as he had never been before and had emerged completely vindicated.

While the pain of this incident never really left either Jack or Annette. To a great extent the violation they endured scarred them, but Garden Fresh was able to move forward with newfound resolve.

It wasn't long before we'd need that resolve.

FORGIVENESS

One of those two customers that Chuck and Dave initially secured from Garden Fresh was Basha Foods.

Basha was a suburban Detroit hummus manufacturer that was making a terrific product and was the leading brand in southeastern Michigan.

Chuck actually worked at Basha prior to moving over to Garden Fresh. At the time Garden Fresh was producing a fresh salsa for Basha.

Everyone involved agreed that Chuck moving from Basha to Garden Fresh was a good idea and an arrangement was entered into; Basha would purchase any fresh salsa it ever distributed from Garden Fresh.

Similarly, if Garden Fresh ever wanted to enter the hummus category it would employ Basha as its manufacturer.

Soon, though, the owner of Basha learned that Chuck and Dave were developing a hummus line at Garden Fresh.

Incensed, he called Jack directly. Within hours Jack pulled up in Basha's parking lot in a truck filled with all the ingredients necessary to make hummus in Garden Fresh's possession.

"It was a class act by Jack," the Basha owner has since told me. "I still remember him opening the back of that truck and the look on his face when he realized one of the oil barrels had fallen over and spilled. What a mess."

Still, some semblance of trust had been reached.

Basha's owner was also extremely proficient in what is known as DSD, or direct store delivery. DSD is where a company sends its own driver into a store and packs its product directly onto the shelves, saving the retailer the time and expense of having their own employees do so.

DSD is a complicated and expensive way to get your product to market, but if you can master it the dividends are profound. Having your own employees, who in a DSD system are typically paid by commission, place your product on your customers' shelves is extremely valuable. They'll squeeze more product onto those shelves than a retailer would ever normally do, leaving less room for your competitors' brands.

Basha had expanded their DSD system beyond Detroit and into Chicago, where they were growing rapidly, particularly with respect to Garden Fresh Salsa. In fact, they were distributing Garden Fresh to one of metro Chicago's largest accounts, Jewel Supermarkets, and had just purchased two new trucks to handle the volume.

Out of nowhere Basha's owner received a call from one of his drivers. Apparently a new Chicago-based food broker Garden Fresh had hired, unbeknown to Jack, had scored a meeting with Jewel and Jewel had decided to start purchasing Garden Fresh Salsa directly from Garden Fresh and not via Basha's DSD system.

Thus, when Chuck and Dave reached out to Basha to let Buddies Foods make fresh salsa for them, Basha's owner agreed.

"I was vulnerable at that moment," Basha's owner has since told me. "And they knew it."

For the next 18 months, about the only communication between Garden Fresh and Basha was via our respective attorneys.

Garden Fresh filed a lawsuit against Basha to prevent Basha from purchasing salsa from Buddies Foods and prevailed.

Tremendous acrimony was still present between the two camps, and soon Garden Fresh's production managers decided to stop filling Basha's fresh salsa orders.

Basha sued Garden Fresh to force them to fill the orders, and this time Basha prevailed.

It was at this time that I began to interject myself into the situation.

I told Jack I was going to schedule a meeting with Basha's owner, in his office, just to see whether we could begin working together in a more constructive fashion.

"Good luck with that," was all Jack could say.

I went into the meeting with an open mind and was surprised by what I found.

Sitting across the table from me was an entrepreneur who, just like Jack and me, had started with virtually nothing and was also trying as best he could to find his place in this world.

I absolutely identified with all that.

Just as I entered his office with an open mind, he took the meeting with an open heart, readily admitting to me mistakes he had made and things he wished he could do over, such as agreeing to work with Buddies Foods in the first place.

He was surprisingly mature, not at all like the villain he was at times made out to be by our lawyers.

The more I listened to him and tried to fully comprehend his point of view, the more I understood why he did what he did and that he was not solely to blame for all that had transpired between our two firms.

In fact, Garden Fresh bore some responsibility as well.

That meeting was the genesis of a relationship between the two of us born out of professional respect, and it soon grew into personal friendship as well.

So much so that as the legal issues between Basha and Garden Fresh wound down, Basha's owner insisted that any future interactions he had with Garden Fresh were to be exclusively with me. He even had his attorney add a line into our respective companies' settlement principles stating just that.

To illustrate just how constructively we were able to work together after that initial meeting, Basha's owner did testify on behalf of Garden Fresh at the Buddies Foods trial, even though his wife is related to Chuck's spouse.

Even a gesture as gracious as that, however, and even as well as Basha's owner and I were working together, were not enough to completely erase from everyone's minds all the pain of the past. All the lawsuits, the subsequent court appearances, the hundreds of thousands of dollars in legal fees, had all taken their inexorable toll.

Thus, when I approached the Garden Fresh management group with the idea that we should buy Basha Foods, to say their reaction was mixed would be an understatement.

"Absolutely not," was the consensus.

I absolutely understood where they were coming from. The drama of the past few years were scarring events, particularly for Jack and Annette.

In fact, Annette said she was unable to trust anyone for years. At this time she was in no position to trust the owner of Basha Foods.

On which the balance of the Garden Fresh management group was in complete agreement.

With one exception: Jack.

Deep down Jack knew that we at Garden Fresh had made our fair share of mistakes, too. And deep down Jack had a profound respect for all the owner of Basha Foods had gone through to build his business.

Jack saw how well I was working with Basha's owner. He also saw how strategically sound this decision was for Garden Fresh. If we were going to be a full-service deli supply company, we simply could not ignore the hummus market any longer.

Not only did we not know how to make hummus, but we couldn't make hummus and salsa in the same plant anyway, for reasons having to do with food safety—there were serious cross-contamination issues involving ingredients employed to make hummus that could not come into contact with our fresh salsa.

As a result we needed a separate plant to make hummus. We needed a company that was already generating volume to justify the expense of entering the hummus market to our bankers.

Buying Basha Foods not only made perfect business sense, but it was in essence our only option.

So Jack said yes, despite the screams forthcoming from virtually all our professional advisors as well as most of his family.

Closing the deal was extremely contentious, as Jack and I had little cooperation from the balance of our management team, a sentiment we completely understood, so we just worked around it.

But close the deal we did, on May 1st, 2006. Jack and I were in the car together heading back to Garden Fresh directly afterward and we barely said a word to each other; we were both too exhausted and simply needed the time to decompress.

Six months later, however, we launched our Garden Fresh Gourmet branded hummus line.

To this day, the now former owner of Basha Foods is a dear friend of Garden Fresh and knows he is welcome in any of our plants or offices at any time.

And he no longer needs to be accompanied by his attorney.

RESPECT AND DIGNITY

Jack, Annette, and I had just landed at New York's LaGuardia airport. I was in the front seat of the cab heading into Manhattan. They were in back; when I turned around to check on them, neither of them looked particularly happy.

That night I took them to Jack's favorite restaurant in the city, Tribeca Grill, and noticed Annette was near tears. Jack was pretty shook up, too.

"Guys," I said. "What's wrong with this picture? We're here to finalize a deal with one of the largest food companies in the world. Think of all we've been through; I started my company on my girlfriend's credit card loan; you two started Garden Fresh in the back of a bankrupt restaurant. Selling to Pepsi is our American dream coming true. Why is this so hard?"

And as big as Pepsi was, they were not the biggest company we had been in discussions to sell Garden Fresh to; a year earlier an even larger food company, Nestlé, had approached us.

Nestlé held a majority stake in a premier Israeli hummus manufacturer, a company called Osem. Osem produces the second largest brand of hummus in Israel, Tzabar.

"Tzabar" is Hebrew for "Sabra."

In the early 1990s an Israeli immigrant living in New York decided to launch his own hummus company. He subsequently petitioned Osem for the North American rights to the name "Sabra."

Osem, figuring hummus would never catch on in the United States, saw this as an easy way to make some money and sold the name "Sabra" to him into perpetuity for a one-time fee of $250,000.

Well, fast forward 15 years or so and hummus had exploded onto the American food scene, even surpassing fresh salsa in terms of category size. In addition, it was still growing faster than fresh salsa.

Furthermore, this upstart Israeli immigrant had built Sabra into the largest brand of hummus in America.

So then he sells his company to Osem's largest competitor in Israel, a company called Strauss, who just happens to own the largest brand of hummus in Israel.

Thus, Nestlé's Osem division finds itself in an unfortunate position; it's the number 2 brand of hummus in it's homeland and its arch enemy, who owns the number 1 brand of hummus in its homeland, just bought the number 1 brand of hummus in the world's largest market.

By the way, in the United States your arch enemy is employing your own brand name, Sabra, that you sold for what now appears to be a song about a decade and a half ago.

That's akin to Pepsi selling the rights, forever, to "Diet Pepsi" to some upstart in China, and then having the Coca-Cola Company purchase the company Pepsi sold those rights to after they became the dominant brand in China.

To add to Osem's grief, after purchasing Sabra Hummus, Strauss sold half their interest to Pepsi and entered into a 75-year joint venture with them.

So now Osem is competing not just against its personal public enemy number 1 but also against the largest food company in America, Pepsi Cola, and their dominant sales, marketing, and distribution resources.

Once Pepsi entered the picture, they brought in their own executive team and pretty much cleaned out Sabra's executive suite.

Sensing an opportunity, Jack reached out to Sabra's former president and brought him in as Garden Fresh's chief operating officer.

All this took place just after we purchased the Basha Hummus Company. That's when Jack and our new COO hopped on a plane to Israel and came back with $1.9 million worth of equipment to make hummus in the authentic Mediterranean fashion, using dried chickpeas that are roasted, whipped into a mash, cured overnight, and then added to a hopper with other ingredients the next day to make hummus.

The company that brought this authentic Mediterranean manufacturing method to the United States?

Sabra Hummus Company.

So the same man who had set up Sabra's manufacturing processes in New York was now Garden Fresh's chief operating officer and was guiding us to make hummus in this same ancient fashion. No cutting corners and using canned chickpeas, as virtually every other U.S. manufacturer was doing. Instead, Garden Fresh was matching, if not surpassing, the quality of the best selling hummus in America.

The new Garden Fresh COO was friends with some people at Osem. When he told them that he was now working for Garden Fresh, Osem sensed an opportunity.

By purchasing Garden Fresh, Osem would gain entry into the U.S. market, capture the largest fresh salsa brand in this country, a category Strauss/Pepsi were not even into yet, and be able to compete with their arch enemy in the deli with both salsa and hummus. And with chips and dips, too, two other categories the Frito-Lay/Strauss joint venture were not competing in yet.

The chairman of Osem reached out to us and asked whether he and his president could come to Detroit to talk to us. We said sure, particularly after learning that they were predominantly owned by Nestlé. We figured big companies are very capable of writing big checks.

Their president came in first, and I picked him up at Detroit's airport after he had flown in from Tel Aviv.

Talk about a guy not well versed in the art of winning friends and influencing people.

We had barely said "hi" to each other in the car, and for virtually the entire ride to our plant he's peppering me with questions regarding the size of the U.S. salsa and hummus market. He was fighting every answer I gave him with data of his own. Where he got all this data I was not sure, but I was sure virtually all of it was wrong.

When we finally got to Garden Fresh, we walked into our building and I settled him into our conference room.

Within a couple minutes Jack and Annette walked in. The first thing this guy said to Jack was: "In my country your plant would be shut down right now."

He proceeded to say that he had witnessed a couple Garden Fresh employees in the parking lot on their break wearing their lab coats.

Tears started filling Annette's eyes. Jack handled it with his usual aplomb, but I could tell right away this was not going to go well.

The next morning I picked the Osem president up from his hotel. He came down 45 minutes late and told me he was on a conference call, but did not even offer an apology. Frankly, he acted as if I was lucky to get an explanation out of him.

On the way to our plant I asked him if he wanted to stop at Starbucks.

"Sure," he replied. "I haven't had any coffee today."

In line at Starbucks, he turned around and said to me: "You know, in Israel this place would not last six months. Starbucks coffee sucks."

Later that day, Osem's chairman arrived. Talk about a contrast in styles.

The chairman was tall and dignified with a regal, elegant sense of style. He spoke slowly with a deep baritone voice. He had a commanding presence; you couldn't help but be engaged in what he was saying.

Even more importantly, he spoke to us respectfully—the antithesis of his president.

We had dinner that night, and multiple other visits soon followed.

One morning he and I were having breakfast alone at his hotel. "I have fallen in love with Garden Fresh," he told me. "I want to come back next week and make an offer on behalf of Nestlé Foods and Osem."

We certainly were going to listen to what the largest food company in the world would offer for Garden Fresh, so we set up a meeting for the following week.

The chairman flew back to Detroit the evening prior to our meeting. I picked him up from the airport and, while we were in the car heading to his hotel, the first thing he said was: "Tribe is for sale, you know."

Tribe was the second leading brand of hummus in the United States, behind Sabra. And yes, I did know they were for sale, and I told him so.

What struck me more than anything else is that he'd even bring the subject up, as if he was trying to ensure that I not negotiate with him, that I just accept whatever he offered, as he had other options in the market to pursue.

I thought to myself: "We're not even formally for sale; you guys approached us. We're hardly motivated sellers who are just going to take whatever offer you put on the table."

The next day we all gathered in our lawyer's oversized confer- ence room. The Osem chairman was there, along with his president, as well as the entire Garden Fresh contingent, including our lawyer, accountant, and financial advisor. Jack even had a couple of his kids come.

After some dutiful pleasantries, the chairman announced that he had been given permission by the Osem board and by the powers that be at Nestlé to make the following offer.

But rather than just let us know what that offer was, he instead launched into an uninterrupted 25-minute diatribe detailing his career at Osem, their sale to Nestlé, all that Osem and Nestlé had done together, even mentioning his 44-foot catamaran that he docked in Barcelona.

It just went on and on and on. Even his president was losing interest and was just staring down at the blank legal pad in front of him.

Finally, a number came out of his mouth: $15.0 million for 50.1 per- cent of Garden Fresh.

We were shocked at how low the offer was. Garden Fresh was on the verge of doing $46 million in sales that year, and here he was valuing us at about half that amount. A value at approximately one and half times our sales would have been appropriate.

Frankly, it was a complete waste of everyone's time. He really should have just called us on the phone and saved himself a trip in from Tel Aviv.

Just as the chairman announced the figure, the Osem president's eyes darted up from his legal pad and in my direction. He was obvi- ously trying to gauge my reaction.

I never did get around to asking him whether he could tell by the look on my face the offer was a non-starter.

I tried to be as gracious as I could, though, and thanked them for their interest, told them we'd need some time to think about it, which they understood and left the meeting to retreat back to their hotel.

When the Garden Fresh contingent was back together in our lawyer's conference room, we couldn't help but laugh at what had just transpired.

Within minutes we were all in agreement: the offer was not even worth countering.

Frankly, not only was it not enough money, but we simply did not have the comfort level to be associated with these people. In essence, we'd be giving up our independence and working for them, as they wanted a majority stake in Garden Fresh.

We subsequently met the next morning and explained that we had decided to remain independent and would not be countering their offer.

The Osem chairman was very surprised and asked Jack: "Are you sure?"

Without missing a beat, Jack, after saying that if we took their offer we'd subsequently own a minority share in Garden Fresh, said: "I already have one boss, and she's sitting right next to me. I certainly don't need another."

Of course he meant Annette, who was sitting right next to him.

I'm not convinced, though, that Jack's sense of humor connected with their Israeli sensibilities, and their shock soon turned to dismay. As our general counsel was ushering them out of our plant, the Osem president told him: "You'll regret this" and "You'll be seeing us in the market-place."

Sure enough we soon did. Osem/Nestlé did indeed move forward and purchased Tribe Hummus Company, the second largest brand in the United States.

So now we found ourselves competing with the Israeli division of the largest food company in the world, Nestlé.

We knew it would not be long before they started employing their resources to secure slots next to ours on retailers' shelves. As well as launch a national advertising campaign, something we'd probably never be in a position to do.

About this same time, Jack and Annette's youngest son, Daniel, would be graduating from high school. So Jack and Annette were about to become empty-nesters.

Jack and I had previously discussed that that would be an opportune time to sell Garden Fresh, so that he and Annette could devote more time to traveling.

Coupling that with Nestlé/Osem purchasing Tribe Hummus Company, and sensing that Garden Fresh was becoming increasingly vulnerable from a competitive standpoint, I approached Jack with the notion of us seeing whether Pepsi would be interested in buying us.

Jack thought it was a great idea and encouraged me to see what I could put together.

I reached out to a local Detroit-based retail executive who used to deal with Pepsi, and he contacted an old friend of his at Pepsi's Frito-Lay unit. Frito-Lay was Pepsi's snack division and had entered into the 75-year joint venture with Strauss and purchased 50 percent of Sabra from them.

A couple years before that, Frito-Lay had purchased Stacy's Pita Chips, and now they were the number 1 brand of pita chips in the United States.

And Stacy's was merchandised in the deli, just like Sabra, and just like Garden Fresh. Thus, I sensed we'd be an ideal strategic fit for Pepsi/Frito-Lay/Strauss.

Upon hearing the idea, they thought so too and invited me to Pepsi's Purchase, New York, world headquarters, where I put on a two-hour-and-15-minute presentation to the Frito-Lay/Strauss Joint Venture board.

The notion of adding to their leadership position in the deli by adding the leading brand of fresh salsa in the United States, along with a major hummus and dip manufacturer, appealed to them—and greatly.

Soon they put together a team, consisting of four Frito-Lay executives and four Strauss executives, to intently study purchasing Garden Fresh. Another presentation to them ensued, this time at our accountant's office in Detroit, followed by waves of processing engineers flowing through our plants to study our operations.

Finally, an offer arrived. This time, however, via fax followed by a conference call—no endless soliloquy with details of yachts anchored in Spain.

The second largest food company in the world was now offering us $60 million, with $40 million paid in cash at closing and another $20 million if we hit certain sales targets within 18 months.

Jack asked me if I thought I could hit those sales targets, and I told him I didn't think we'd have any problem doing so. We were still growing at a very rapid pace.

So we agreed to continue the dialogue with the Frito-Lay/Strauss joint venture.

It wasn't always an easy dialogue to continue, though.

First, we soon learned that the joint venture was about to build a new hummus manufacturing factory in Virginia. We assumed they would shut down our Michigan-based plants and move our Garden Fresh production out of state.

Second, as with the Osem guys from Nestlé, we found the Strauss contingent to be challenging to deal with. They were routinely argumentative with us and did not seem to trust their own partners.

In fact, one Strauss executive called me at home one Sunday evening to ask if Frito-Lay executives were having private conversations with me. They were not, and I told him so, but he acted as if he did not believe me.

"We think they want this deal so much that they're saying one thing to us and another thing to you so that we'll pay more," he told me. I tried to reassure him that I was not witnessing any evidence of that. He finally said, "OK, and you're not going to tell him that I called you, right?"

I told him I would not, and I never did.

On top of all this, trying to finalize the formal terms of their offer was agonizing.

One day, while I was "technically" on spring break with my family in Scottsdale, after a seemingly endless flurry of calls I noticed my cell phone was hot to the touch. I checked my registry and counted them; I had just hit 60 calls. And it was only noon.

A week later I was in Seattle and on a conference call with the Frito-Lay contingent, who were in suburban Dallas at their corporate head-quarters, and with the Strauss group, which was in Israel.

I was about to tell them about a refinement to their offer we were going to request when one of the Strauss executives said, "Look, why don't we all just get together around a table and discuss these issues, once and for all. How does the week after next in New York look like for everybody?"

I thought it was a terrific idea, and everyone cleared their schedules to meet in a hotel conference room in Times Square in two weeks.

Thus, Jack, Annette, and I found ourselves in the Tribeca Grill the evening before our meeting.

"Look, guys," I said to them. "If this is this hard for you, we don't have to do it. We have not agreed to anything. We're perfectly free to walk away."

"No," Jack replied. "This is too much money. This will take care of our family for generations to come. I want you to go into that meeting tomorrow and put this deal together for us."

Knowing Jack as well as I did, I knew his head was saying one thing to me, but his heart was saying something else. If that wasn't enough, Annette looked completely crestfallen.

"Why don't we sleep on it tonight and see how we feel in the morning," I told them. "We don't have to decide this very moment."

The next morning we met in the hotel lobby. I told Jack I'd take them to his favorite Manhattan breakfast spot, the Carnegie Deli—Jack loves their pastrami omelette.

We hadn't even made it out to the street before I noticed Annette wiping tears from her face. Jack's eyes were bloodshot, too. I doubt either of them slept much that night.

Once we were seated at the restaurant, I did not have to ask them how they felt, so I just continued the conversation from the prior evening.

"Jack, Annette, this is still our company. We haven't signed anything binding yet. We don't have to sell if the two of you don't want to—we'll be fine."

Without hesitation, Jack said to me: "Thank you, Dave, but we've spent almost the entire night talking about this. I want you to go into that room and put together the best deal you can for us."

So from there we were off to the Times Square hotel, where we met up with our general counsel, our outside attorney, our accountant, and our financial advisor.

From there we took the elevator up to the designated conference room, where the Frito-Lay team, who had arrived from Dallas the day before, were already seated around the table with the Strauss group, who had flown in from Israel.

What I had wanted to convey in that conference call two weeks prior, when I was in Seattle and the Frito-Lay/Strauss contingency was in Dallas and Israel, was that we were going to counter their offer.

Specifically, instead of $60 million total with $40 million due at closing and the other $20 million due in 18 months if we hit certain sales goals, we were now asking for $44 million down and the balance of $16 million due in only 12 months if we hit those same sales goals.

In other words, increase the up-front money by 10 percent, or $4 million, and reduce the time we had to earn the balance by 33 percent, moving from 18 months to only 12.

I thought then, and still do to this day, that this counter was actually in the Frito-Lay/Strauss joint venture's best interests.

I figured: What was another $4 million up-front to these guys? They'd eventually pay that anyway, as we were still growing rapidly and would most certainly realize at least that much of our earn out potential.

In terms of reducing the length of the earn out if we did not hit our sales targets, they'd eventually pay less than the $60 million they were committing to, which would be good news for them. If we did hit our target, they'd get a bigger company faster than they expected, which would also be good news for them.

After this was all conveyed to them, the looks on the faces of the Frito-Lay executives suggested to me "this sounds reasonable."

But before I could even canvass the faces of the Strauss group to see how they were processing this information, their lead executive was pounding his fist on the conference table.

"What is this all about?" he thundered. "You're changing our deal? We flew in all the way from Israel for this?"

Everyone was shocked, even his partners from Frito-Lay. This, after all, was the purpose of this meeting in the first place, to finalize terms of the deal. This meeting was the Strauss group executive's idea: to discuss this in person as opposed to via the phone.

Everyone in the room, both the Garden Fresh contingency and the Frito-Lay group, tried to calm him down, but to no avail. He just kept getting angrier and angrier.

After about 15 minutes or so, one of the Frito-Lay executives suggested they all go out in the hall to discuss the situation privately among themselves. We readily said yes—anything to break the tension.

As they were all out in the hall, we couldn't help but talk amongst ourselves about how ridiculous his behavior was. It just came out of nowhere. We felt like we were in a scene from a movie.

After about 10 minutes, the Frito-Lay/Strauss group re-entered the room. After sitting down, the lead Strauss executive, while noticeably calmer, would not change his tune. "We flew all the way to New York from Israel," he continued, "thinking we had a deal. Now within minutes of sitting down you're changing the deal. We did not come here to change this deal. Either you take our offer or you leave it."

Instantly and instinctively, Annette announced: "Well then, we're leaving it. Let's go, everyone."

With that we all simply packed our briefcases, calmly shook everyone's hands, and walked out of the conference room to the elevator.

I'm not sure whether they thought this maneuver was a stunt on our part and we'd return after realizing what we were walking away from, but we simply left the hotel.

When we got out to Times Square, Jack said, "A minute ago I was staring $60 million in the face. Now I've got $16 million in debt instead. And you know what? I've never been happier. Let's go eat!"

So I hailed our driver and took everyone out to one of my favorite Manhattan restaurants, Gramercy Tavern.

To this day, Jack and Annette refer to that day as one of the happiest of their lives.

Annette told me she never really wanted to sell in the first place; she was simply trusting Jack's judgment that this time was best for them. Furthermore, and most importantly, once she heard Pepsi was building that new plant in Virginia and that all our current Garden Fresh employees would lose their jobs, selling the company was almost an unbearable thought for her, at any price.

Jack told me that, in the back of the cab when we were first going to our hotel in Manhattan, it first hit him: "I'm not going to own this company any more." He said that the feeling he had when walking out of that conference room was "like when I was a kid and would get out of school for the summer."

My feelings were mixed.

Personally, I had grown close to the Frito-Lay executives and regretted that our deal ended the way it did, with such a total meltdown by their partners. There are more reasons why deals of this nature do not close than why they do close, and I understand that. So many things have to be in alignment to actually get a deal done, but for this deal to end is this fashion was a shame to me. I would have preferred a more dignified exit on their behalf.

Professionally, it was not lost on me that, moving forward, our world would be much more difficult. We now had walked away from offers from the two largest food companies in the world—very serious, very aggressive people with resources we could only dream of possessing. They were not simply going to walk away from the deli space just because we walked away from them.

In fact, it was not long before the Frito-Lay/Strauss joint venture purchased the number 3 and number 5 brands of fresh salsa in the country.

But that would all have to wait. For the time being, I was simply going to savor my favorite dish at Gramercy Tavern, their luscious sea bass.

COMPASSION

Is it possible for a company's bond with its hometown to be so strong that it's eventually considered a family member? I believe it is. And I believe Garden Fresh did just that.

When Garden Fresh first got into Costco, we decided to donate part of our proceeds to the Children's Hospital in Detroit. We actually put their logo on the back of our labels, the first company to ever do that for them.

Soon Costco was Garden Fresh's largest customer, so our monthly checks were starting to capture the attention of the hospital's development officer.

She reached out and invited me to tour the facility with her.

As we were walking the halls, I noticed other companies had secured naming rights to a reading room or a play area, so I asked if that might be in the cards for Garden Fresh.

I figured maybe we could get a broom closet or something, but a week later she called me back and asked, "How does the 'Garden Fresh Healing Garden' sound to you?"

It turns out the Detroit Children's Hospital was the only top-ten pediatric care facility in the nation that did not have an outdoor garden for family members to retreat to while their children are being treated.

I thought a "Garden Fresh Healing Garden" sounded great, and after a short meeting at the hospital learned that they'd need $185,000 from Garden Fresh to make it happen.

My meeting with Jack and Annette to run the proposal by them was even shorter.

"Sure," Jack said. "Let's do it."

Within a year, the Garden Fresh Healing Garden at Detroit's Children's Hospital formally opened, with an 18-foot yellow ribbon designed by our chief creative officer, Mike Griffin, signaling its entrance.

As it turned out, any conversation I had with Jack involving anything to do with a charity never lasted long.

So many companies engage in charitable activities not so much out of altruism but as a social obligation.

Not Jack. His feeling was that we were indebted to the community.

"It just feels normal," he'd tell me. "We're lucky to be able to do this."

So when Jimmy Buffett's Margaritaville Enterprises' charitable arm, "Singing for Change," asked me to be on their advisory board, Jack replied: "I hope you said yes."

Soon thereafter, Singing for Change, which donates $1 from every Jimmy Buffet concert ticket to charities in the cities he performs in, was making $25,000 donations to Detroit-based best-selling author Mitch Albom's charities. They were Mitch's largest single payments.

Jack completely supported me joining the executive board of the largest food rescue mission in the United States, an organization called Forgotten Harvest.

Soon after, we applied our licensing expertise garnered from our Margaritaville experience and developed a similar program for them. Today Forgotten Harvest has more than 35 branded products for sale in and around Detroit. It's a program that could revolutionize philanthropy in this country, as it both increases the charity's visibility and provides a new revenue stream as food manufacturers pay a royalty for the use of their names.

Before long, Jack was giving so much to the local Boys and Girls Club, after learning how much higher graduation rates were for the kids who belonged, that they named a wing after him and Annette.

Also, Jack and Annette's donations to the Detroit area Salvation Army were so generous that he was awarded a seat on their national board.

And these were just a few of the major charitable activities Garden Fresh participated in. In addition, there were countless local events, civic organizations that never had to ask Garden Fresh twice to support them.

The result was there was an unmistakable aura to Garden Fresh in the metro Detroit community. Yes, we were an "Only in America" story that you just could not help but root for, and yes our products were inherently fun and simply put a smile on your face. Those who knew we had grown to become the number 1 brand of fresh salsa in the United States were genuinely proud of a local company that had gone national.

But there was more to the aura than all that. Jack's inherent giving nature created a bond with the people of southeastern Michigan that was genuinely special, and virtually impossible to replicate. It resulted in a mysterious sense of goodwill for us; Garden Fresh was truly beloved.

VALUES *ARE* VALUABLE

Ten years after the Buddies Foods trial ended, Jack and I were in an airport, just after exhibiting at the national deli show in Orlando. As we were waiting to board our flight back to Detroit, up walked Chuck and Dave themselves. They too had exhibited at the show and were on our same flight back home.

To their credit, both Chuck and Dave could not have been more gracious. Chuck was genuine in his remorse and asked for forgiveness. Dave called betraying Jack and Annette and Garden Fresh "the worst thing I've ever done in my life."

My sixth sense told me they were speaking from the heart and speaking from a moral perspective regarding what they had done to launch their company under such false pretenses.

But as I was flying back to Detroit I just could not help but think: those two cost themselves enormous sums of money by not taking the honorable route and staying with Jack and Annette. They could have owned 10 percent of Garden Fresh, a stake that is vastly more valuable than Buddies Foods, a company that is still relatively small and by all accounts struggling.

As it turned out, Garden Fresh was not an easy company for them to compete against, even when in possession of our own recipes.

And whenever I talk to the now former owner of Basha Foods, he reminds me of just how grateful he is that he sold his company to Garden Fresh. Not only was he burned out at the time and struggling with work/ life balance issues, but the money he realized from the sale, and we paid him the exact price that he had negotiated with Sabra, has allowed him to live the life he truly imagined for himself.

It was not long before Garden Fresh was the third largest hummus manufacturer in the United States, and to this day hummus comprises close to 40 percent of Garden Fresh's total sales.

None of that would have been possible without genuine forgiveness being exhibited by everyone involved.

While Garden Fresh's charitable endeavors were never, ever done for business purposes, it was tremendous for business.

I truly believe whenever one of our customers was faced with a choice between Garden Fresh and one of our competitors, if all other things were equal, they'd gravitate toward the brand that ceaselessly devoted itself to those less fortunate among us.

The year after we walked out of that hotel conference room in Times Square, ending our deal with the Pepsi/Frito-Lay/Strauss joint venture, I received an unsolicited call from the new vice president of mergers and acquisitions at Frito-Lay.

He was an absolute class act personally, and brilliant, I thought, professionally. He was Ivy League–educated, worked for Pepsi for years, then left for a stint at the stellar business consulting firm McKinsey & Company.

He had just returned to Pepsi when the VP of M&A position opened up at Frito-Lay. He moved his family from New York to Dallas and asked if I'd meet him there for dinner.

At dinner he told me the consensus at Frito-Lay was that letting the Garden Fresh group walk out of that conference room in New York was one of the biggest strategic mistakes Frito-Lay had made in the past five years.

He was not with the company when it all happened, but he had been informed that, if it had been up to the Americans, they would have taken my reasonable counteroffer. The Frito-Lay guys just could not settle their Strauss partners down long enough to make a deal, and their emotions simply got the best of them. And then we walked out, never to return.

He subsequently asked me whether there was any way we could revive the discussions.

I told him we had grown so much in the past year that the price that was on the table was no longer of any interest to us. In addition, there were probably too many other complicating factors, such as their new plant in Virginia that would have resulted in all our employees losing their jobs, for a deal between our respective entities to be consummated.

As it turned out, even with the Frito-Lay/Strauss joint venture, which was then two years into it's 75-year term, eventually buying two of the top five fresh salsa brands in the United States, as well as launching a Sabra brand of fresh salsa, they never did overtake Garden Fresh's number 1 position in sales.

Neither of us knew then, though, that that would be the case.

But I did leave him with one final thought: "Don't worry too much about being associated with the Strauss guys; you've only got 73 years left, and then you're home free."

Secret 6: Do You Value Values?

Values do shape, and eventually become, your destiny.

At Garden Fresh we valued our place in this world, to be the best, and never wavered in our determination to preserve our best-in class flavor profile.

Sometimes, though, you don't know you have a value until you're tested.

Jack came out of the Chuck and Dave's trial stronger than when he went in. As painful as the experience was, in the end he found the resolve to defend what was rightfully his.

Sometimes values emerge through adversity.

Listening, empathizing, and building relationships with the owner of Basha Hummus allowed us to finally end our differences and accomplish something truly special.

Continued

Continued

Sometimes you realize your values are not in alignment with those who want to be associated with you.

That was the case with both Nestle' and Pepsi. We chose to walk away from both.

What are your values?

What are your company's values?

Are they in alignment?

The more aligned your company is with your values, the more authentic your offerings will be.

And the more value you'll create.

7

If a Fortune 500 Company Calls, Take the Call

All's Well That Ends Well

—*William Shakespeare*

What's it like to sell your startup to a Fortune 500 Company? What is the actual process involved? What twists and turns do you encounter along the way? How do you arrive at a price?

We didn't know it at the time, but we were about to find out. It would turn out to be our biggest adventure of all.

Jack and I were invited to be the keynote speakers at the 2014 Michigan Grocers Association's annual meeting. The event was held in the impossibly gorgeous northern Michigan town of Traverse City, about a four-hour commute from Detroit.

We were driving up in Jack's enormous GMC Yukon Denali. When you're 6-feet 5-inches tall, you need all the room you can get, and this thing had every bell and whistle you can imagine, plus tons of storage spaces, seemingly everywhere. I was behind the wheel, as I usually was when we were on long trips in the car together, so that Jack could take his occasional nap.

Just before dozing off he says to me: "Lift up the door to that compartment." I did and was both startled and a bit mortified.

"You're packing heat?"

There was a huge Glock resting there.

"Yeah. You know it just makes me feel more secure. I bought three of them, and Annette and I are going to shooting ranges a couple times a week. She's actually getting pretty good at it."

Knowing Jack as I did, I remember saying to myself: "This isn't going to be good for anybody."

I noticed the gun discussion perked him up a bit so I just thought I'd make some small talk.

"I'm curious," I asked him. "What do you think we're worth?"

"What?" he replied. "Garden Fresh?"

"Yeah," I responded. Food company valuations were at historical highs. General Mills, in fact, had just bought a company called Annie's Naturals for four times revenue, which would put Garden Fresh's corresponding value in the $400 million range.

"Oh," he said, as he started to recline his seat back so he could comfortably fall asleep. "I'd say, when it's all said and done, about $40 million."

I was as stunned as when I first saw the Glock.

"Jack," I said. "I wouldn't let you sell this company for $140 million. Didn't you hear about the Annie's Naturals deal?"

I had actually been following Annie's Naturals for a while. They had created a brand whose proposition was to offer traditional children's products, like mac-n-cheese, in all natural and often organic formats. The premise was that parents could still provide these time-honored treats to their kids but not feel guilty doing so, as they wouldn't be shoving preservatives and the like down their throats.

I had been so impressed with how Wall Street was valuing Annie's Naturals that I had proposed to Jack and Annette that we change our brand from Garden Fresh *Gourmet* to Garden Fresh *Naturals*. I believed our branding was better than Annie's Naturals and that our packaging was superior, too. I knew our products tasted better, and we made all our own items, whereas Annie's outsourced all their manufacturing. Our categories were growing faster as well.

Thus, I thought we could unlock some value from our brand by having our actual name emphasize the all natural nature of our products.

To illustrate what a joy it is to be associated with Jack, when I initially ran the idea by him, we discussed it back and forth for maybe a minute, emphasis on maybe, and he simply said, "Sounds good. Let's do it."

I remember thinking: "This would only happen in a bootstrapping entrepreneurial company, never in corporate America; we just decided in 60 seconds to change the name of our company. No research, no focus groups, just following our instincts."

Jack was in full reclining mode now, about ready to doze off, and said: "That's nice. I'm happy for Annie."

I didn't have the heart to tell him that there was no "Annie," at least not anymore. The company had been bought years ago by a private equity firm, which had subsequently taken it public.

Instead, I just let Jack fall asleep.

BEEN THERE, DONE THAT. SO WHAT? DO IT AGAIN

Selling Garden Fresh might have been on my mind due to a meeting I had coming up in a couple weeks. I had been contacted, unsolicited, by a Fortune 500 company that was expressing interest in us.

I hadn't even told Jack and Annette about it; these things happened to us so often they weren't even worthy of bringing it up to them anymore.

And frankly, I no longer took these meetings very seriously either. They were really nothing more than glorified networking opportunities for us. You can never have too many friends in this world, I figured.

A year earlier I had spoken at an investment banking conference in New York. It was held at the Marriott Marquis in Times Square.

About the only thing memorable about the event was the room they gave me. Actually "room" would be an understatement; rather, it was a 1,200-square-foot apartment, complete with formal dining for eight and a separate master suite.

Best of all, it was on the 44th floor with a genuine "only in New York" view.

Directly after my presentation, the vice president for mergers and acquisitions for the Campbell Soup Company spoke. Campbell's had just purchased a company called Bolthouse Farms out of Bakersfield, California, for a price that had raised a lot of eyebrows in the food industry.

Then Campbell's VP of M&A and I were on a panel together, and we chatted for a short while afterward.

I had to cut short our conversation as I needed to leave the conference to catch a flight to Bentonville, Arkansas. I had a meeting with Wal-Mart the next morning. There was some major event in Bentonville that day, so the only hotel room my administrative assistant could find me was some dilapidated property on the outskirts of town.

When I got to my room, I opened the shades and looked out the window. All I could see was a gravel parking lot that led to a cornfield. Thinking back to the accommodations I had just enjoyed the night before, and remembering that killer view of Manhattan, about all I could say to myself was: "Oh, how the mighty have fallen."

Months later I received the following e-mail, via LinkedIn, written from an iPad:

Dave,

I am the CEO of Bolthouse Farms, which is a large produce and juice company here in California. Our roots are in Michigan, as that is where we were originally founded about 100 years ago. Mark Stephenson at Meijer is a huge fan of both of our companies and suggested that we might have some synergy in our operations. We have a large HPP capability, as we use it for yogurt-based salad dressing, and a whole series of new products coming to market over the next year. Would you be open to a phone call to bounce some ideas around? We were purchased by the Campbell Soup Company eighteen months ago and are working closely with them to identify growth accelerators, including joint ventures, licensing, and other potential M&A-type activity. The Pepsi/Sabra JV has been really successful, and I wonder if a similar opportunity might exist. Let me know if we can talk.

Jeff Dunn

By this time, April of 2014, Garden Fresh had become a leader in our industry with a national footprint, but still had a long way to go in terms of distribution. As a result we were a very attractive acquisition target and were probably contacted easily twice a month or so in this fashion.

Most people who did reach out to us did so to me, and if someone contacted Jack he would just refer the person to me and not think twice about it.

So I responded to Jeff as follows:

Thanks so much for reaching out, Jeff. Funny but I was a speaker at a conference sponsored by Houlihan Lokey in New York last year and then was on a panel with Campbell's VP of M&A, Ray Liguori—I thought he was terrific.

I appreciate your interest in Garden Fresh and let's try to chat when we get a chance. . . and I'm in California a lot, so maybe we can just meet the next time I'm out there, which will probably be in late May or early June. Enjoy your weekend,

Dave Zilko, Vice Chairman
Garden Fresh Gourmet

What I knew, though, and what Jeff Dunn could not possibly know, was that the owners of Garden Fresh were not even remotely interested in selling the company.

Any time I'd bring the subject up to Jack, he'd just say, "I'll just keep doing this until it's not fun anymore."

And I had never seen Jack and Annette more happy and fulfilled than I had that spring and summer.

What Garden Fresh, the company they had founded in the back of their bankrupt restaurant 17 years ago, had become was nothing short of astonishing: the premier deli supply company in the United States with revenues in excess of $100 million, respected and admired by the largest retailers in the country both for our best-in-class salsa, chips, and hummus and for our desire to form strategic partnerships with them, truly beloved in the metro Detroit community not only for our products but for our endless philanthropic efforts.

All of Jack and Annette's five children worked for the company. Jack would routinely tell visitors to Garden Fresh: "I consider myself the luckiest man in the world. Every day I get to come to work and see all my kids."

We were solidly profitable, so much so that Garden Fresh had stopped becoming about money for us, particularly for Jack and Annette. Jack was certainly no longer taking the bus to work after his car was repossessed—in fact, far from it.

One day he walked into my office and said, "Come on outside with me, I want to show you something."

So I did, and sitting in the parking lot was a brand new yellow Corvette convertible.

"Wow," I said. "When did you decide to do this?"

"About 35 years ago," Jack replied.

"Good for him," I thought. Everyone should be so lucky to get to this point in his or her life when you could fulfill just about every dream you've ever had—when you could truly live the life you've imagined for yourself.

On top of all this, Garden Fresh continued to grow, but at a manageable pace. The days of annual 50 percent increases in revenue were over, frankly because there were no more major retailers left that we were not already selling to, and that was just fine with Jack and Annette. That 50 percent growth pace was brutal to keep up with and brutal gets old really quick.

All in all, things had never been better. In fact, just a couple months earlier Jack and I were discussing whether or not we should have an exit strategy. Jack thought about it for about a second and simply said, "Let's wait and see how I feel when I'm 65," which was in another four years.

So it was in this frame of mind that I proceeded to set up a meeting with Jeff Dunn, the CEO of Bolthouse Farms, an $800 million operation that had recently been purchased, for a very high price, by the Campbell Soup Company, an $8 billion Fortune 500 entity.

To illustrate the sense of urgency, or rather the lack thereof, we had with respect to selling Garden Fresh, I waited another five months before I made it out to Southern California to meet with Jeff.

———

THE FIVE-MINUTE MEET-AND-GREET THAT TURNED INTO A 125-MINUTE MEET-AND-GREET

Two weeks after Jack and my keynote address to the Michigan Association of Grocers Annual Meeting in Traverse City, in which I put on a 40-minute presentation detailing the Garden Fresh miracle and Jack answered questions from the audience for about 15 minutes, I flew to Southern California for three days of meetings.

My first was with Jeff Dunn of Bolthouse Farms. Bolthouse's operations are in Bakersfield, California, a couple hours from LAX, but their administrative offices are in downtown Santa Monica, only about 20 minutes from the airport.

Walking into their office building, I remember thinking to myself that this would be a five-minute meet-and-greet, then I'd be off to my hotel.

Jeff came out to the reception area, greeted me, and led me to their conference room.

Within five minutes, I knew this was going to be a longer meeting than I anticipated.

The connection happened that quickly... virtually instantly. I had never met any other person who felt the same way we did regarding the dynamics of the current trends in the food industry. It was like I was sitting there talking to Jack.

Jeff started out by saying he spent over 20 years with Coca-Cola, rising to president of their North American operations, but eventually realized that this country needed to undergo a food revolution and that he wanted to play a role in changing how people ate. So he moved over to Bolthouse Farms, which focuses on all natural products.

Jack and I always discussed how we wanted to change the way people eat. In fact, that was the major reason why Jack was so interested in HPP, as he believed this was breakthrough technology that could do just that. HPP would allow food companies to offer products in a fresh, all natural format with clean ingredient decks.

Garden Fresh had two HPP machines with a third on the way. Bolthouse had two HPP machines with a third on the way.

Jeff had a vending machine in their conference room, as they were experimenting with selling packets of carrots out of them.

We at Garden Fresh had just bought a vending machine and were experimenting how we might be able to get our dips, salsa, and hummus out of them.

The slogan on the top panel of the Bolthouse Farms vending machine read "Eat It Like Fast Food," which was exactly the intent of our prospective Garden Fresh vending machine program.

Jeff brought out a new product they were working on: a package of fresh carrots, sliced into chips. Inside the bag was a pouch that you pulled, just before consuming, that released a ranch spice blend onto the carrot chips, flavoring them.

I could not help but think back to the time when we were in discussions to sell Garden Fresh to Pepsi and all those Frito-Lay engineers were coming in and laughing at Garden Fresh for using real corn to make our tortilla chips. About how they simply viewed the chip as a delivery vehicle for their best-in-class spice blends, which is where they spent the bulk of their research and development dollars, merely using corn flour for their actual chips.

And now here was Jeff Dunn guy trying to change how people eat by switching out the delivery vehicle from a fried tortilla chip to a fresh carrot chip.

I thought it was a brilliant idea.

I tried the Bolthouse Farms spiced carrot chips, and I thought they were terrific. And only 25 calories per bag. Wow.

Sensing something special was about to happen, I pulled my computer out of my briefcase and asked Jeff whether I could formally introduce Garden Fresh to him. He said sure, and while we were setting it up to project on his screen, he called in two of his C-suite executives: his chief marketing officer and his chief financial and operating officer.

Over the course of the next hour and a half, I detailed for Jeff and his colleagues the entire Garden Fresh saga: from our humble origins in the back of that bankrupt restaurant outside of Detroit, to our leading position in the deli category, to our approach to manufacturing, right down to showing him pictures of the five-gallon buckets in our salsa production facility.

Jeff and his team asked a lot of questions—and they were great questions. I was genuinely impressed.

When it was all said and done, Jeff said something that connected with me to my heart. To my core.

"I love those five-gallon buckets!"

Again I found myself thinking back to our discussions with Nestlé and Pepsi, and how their executives would scoff, politely, if that's even possible, at how we made our salsa. Then they'd proceed to tactfully intimate that it would not be long before they'd come in with their massive capital expenditure budgets and install massive tanks to make our salsa in, just because if you're going to scale national that's just the way real, big, serious food companies do things.

They said it to me in a manner that suggested I should be proud that soon this cute little company we built could finally start to play in the major leagues, with major league production techniques.

But to me our five-gallon buckets were not only the best way to make our Garden Fresh Salsa; I truly believe in micro-batch processing, but they had also become a badge of honor. They symbolized our commitment to making not only a great product but the best product on the market, the best product possible. Even if it resulted in lower margins.

Instead of scoffing at us like the other Fortune 500 companies had, here was a guy running close to a billion-dollar division saying that he got it. He thought that artisanal manufacturing processes, employing a chef's mentality, was where food production in this country was headed. I loved him for saying that.

That was the good news.

The bad news was that we at Garden Fresh did not have an exit strategy, which is what someone who is interested in acquiring you does not want to hear.

I told Jeff just that, but I was so intrigued by the connection I was feeling I did not want to leave it like that.

So thinking as quickly as I could, I said, "But it's not lost on me what General Mills just paid for Annie's Naturals. Four times revenue. If Campbell's is interested in that kind of valuation for Garden Fresh, I'd recommend to Jack and his wife that we seriously consider it.

Jeff responded, "Well, maybe we will."

He then told me he was flying to Camden, New Jersey, the following week to have dinner with the CEO of the Campbell Soup Company, Denise Morrison, and that he'd talk to her about it.

I said that when I got back to Detroit later in the week I'd talk to Jack and Annette about it, too.

Frankly, I don't think Jeff ever intended to have Campbell's pay four times revenue for Garden Fresh and, frankly, I did not think we were worth that much.

But this maneuver on our part allowed us to continue the dialogue, something we were both obviously interested in doing.

So a little more than two hours after I walked into the Bolthouse Farms administrative offices, I found myself on the streets of Santa Monica feeling completely different than when I walked in.

"This is it," I told myself. "These are the people we're going to sell Garden Fresh to."

EVERY IDEA NEEDS A CHAMPION

A few days later, upon returning from California, I ran into Jack in the hallway and told him I needed to speak with him and Annette, as soon as possible.

"Is anything wrong?" he asked.

"No," I replied, "but it's important."

It wasn't until 4:00 that afternoon that the three of us were even in the same building, where we gathered in our Garden Fresh administrative office conference room.

This was the very same conference room where Jack uttered, when a visitor was telling us how much he respected Jack and me because we "started with nothing," his now infamous phrase: "Starting with nothing? That's easy. Try starting with less than nothing. Now, that's hard."

I had to start by telling them that earlier in the year, like five months ago, a division of Campbell's had reached out to me to explore options, options that included buying Garden Fresh. This was such a common occurrence, and I knew we were not even remotely interested in selling, so I never even bothered to tell our Garden Fresh majority owners that a Fortune 500 company had interest in us, let alone that I met with the president and CEO of one of their divisions.

Anyway, I told them about my meeting in Santa Monica with Jeff Dunn and his C-suite team and how impressed I was with them, and what an extraordinary strategic fit I thought we'd be for them.

Immediately, Annette's shoulders slumped and she buried her head in her chest. She then looked up at me and, with tears streaming down her face, she said, "Please, Dave. Don't do this to me again."

Jack had his arms crossed against his chest, and he was shaking his head back and forth: "Dave, we're not for sale. I just don't want to sell."

Not only was I not surprised by their reaction, but I understood it. We had been down this road many times before and were well aware that, as wonderful as the eventual outcome may sound, there's tremendous angst that inevitably lies ahead.

Rumors begin to fly around the office and in the plants, and morale starts to suffer. "We're being bought by a huge company? Will they lay people off? Shut our plant down like Pepsi was going to do?"

Those rumors make their way to the media, too. I remember when we were in the midst of negotiating with Pepsi when a local Detroit radio station broadcast that "local salsa producer Garden Fresh Gourmet has agreed to sell itself to the Coca-Cola Company."

First of all, we had not agreed to sell to anybody, and we were talking to Pepsi, not Coke. Subsequently fielding all the ensuing calls took up the rest of my day and most of the next.

So I told them I understood how they felt, but that while things had never been better within the friendly confines of our company, the outside environment had changed—and changed dramatically, so much so that this was not a situation we could casually shrug off. We had to take this seriously.

I proceeded to tell them about how food company valuations were at historical highs, really starting with Campbell's purchase of Bolthouse Farms a couple years ago and culminated by the stunning price General Mills had just paid for Annie's Naturals: four times revenue, which correlated to a $400 million value for Garden Fresh.

Annette, true to her character, said, "I don't care about the money." I knew she meant she just cared about our employees and their welfare.

I understood that sentiment, too, but I honestly felt that if we did care about our employees we should not just assume that it would always be in their best interests that we own Garden Fresh.

I continued that, as the only Garden Fresh C-suite executive who regularly met with our customers on a national basis, I was starting to sense that market forces were beginning to work against us.

Huge multinational companies had started to enter our deli space. The two biggest food companies in the world that had tried to previously purchase Garden Fresh but could not, Nestlé and Pepsi, were just two examples; after we ended negotiations they both went out and purchased our competitors.

And these companies were outspending us by tens of millions of dollars with national advertising campaigns and other marketing programs. Because of this, it was getting harder and harder for us to keep the shelf space we already had as well as secure new placements.

I told Jack and Annette that we shouldn't assume that Garden Fresh would continue to grow and grow like we always had. I said that while I thought we'd again have record sales of around $110 million in 2014, and that we had a lot coming up in the pipeline for 2015, with our high concentration of customers, if we ever lost one or two, that would be a serious hit for us.

And if that happened we'd be laying people off, for the first time in our history.

I thought we needed to be honest with ourselves and consider that we might have taken this company as far as we could and that the time may have come for us to have access to the resources of a Fortune 500 food company to compete.

Jack then asked: "If we do sell, can we get them to guarantee that they'll keep manufacturing in Michigan?"

I told them that I thought it would be difficult to justify moving our production out of Michigan. Our largest accounts, or at least their shipping depots, were too close to our Midwestern base for it to make any economic sense.

But then I was very clear: "For what they're going to have to pay to buy us, we can't ask them to guarantee anything. Once they own the company, they can do whatever they want, regardless of what they tell us prior to a sale. We all need to understand that, but I'm confident enough in the business case for keeping our manufacturing here in Michigan that they'll do just that."

Finally, Jack asked, "What do you think they'll pay for us?"

I told them that, while the General Mills/Annie's Naturals deal correlated to a value of $400 million for Garden Fresh, I did not think we were worth that much. We simply had not professionalized Garden Fresh to the extent that the private equity firm that had purchased Annie's had.

I told Jack and Annette: "I think we can get somewhere between $200 and $220 million for Garden Fresh, right now. Who knows, maybe as high as $300 million, but if we can get $220 million, that would be a net of $200 million for us, after our $20 million in debt, and if we can get that, I think we should take it."

Both Jack and Annette were still underwhelmed with the entire notion of selling Garden Fresh, and I didn't blame them. We had been down this road many times before, and we were well aware that it's not a fun road to go down.

I finally added: "Look, someday we're going to have to sell this company. And when we do, I can't imagine the two of you being happier than if it ended up in the hands of the people I met earlier this week. You both need to think this over."

Jack said he'd do just that, and that he'd set up a meeting in a few days with his five kids to discuss the matter.

That meeting took place the following Monday. I was not in attendance, but when Jack came out I asked him: "How do you feel? Would you like me to continue the dialogue with Campbell?"

"Yeah. Go ahead," was all he said.

But it was all I needed to hear.

KNOW THE REAL MEANING OF VALUE

Jack's willingness to continue the dialogue was a bit underwhelming, to say the least. While I appreciated how conflicted he and Annette were over selling in general, I truly believed it was in the best interests of Garden Fresh, our employees, for Ferndale, and for the partners, that we seriously consider the opportunity that had just presented itself to us.

I reached out to Jeff Dunn and told him that we were interested in exploring our options with them, and he said he had received permission from Campbell's CEO Denise Morrison to do the same.

Soon we were setting up visits to our Garden Fresh facilities for both the Bolthouse Farms group, based in California, as well as the Campbell's corporate entity, which was headquartered in Camden, New Jersey.

Together they would assess Garden Fresh, determine whether it indeed was a good strategic fit for Campbell's and, if so, subsequently make us an offer.

This meant I was about to be reunited with the vice president of mergers and acquisitions for the Campbell Soup Company, Ray Liguori, with whom I had served on a panel at that investment banking conference in New York.

As we were reconnecting, Ray said, "You may find this strange, but do you know what I remember most about meeting you? Your shoes. I really liked the shoes you had on that day."

More substantive meetings ensued, however. We hosted them for meetings in both October and November, with me putting on presentations on both occasions and Jack providing plant tours as necessary.

One thing quickly became apparent, however: there was tension between the Bolthouse Farms group and Campbell's corporate entity.

Should a sale to Campbell's be consummated, their plan was to have Garden Fresh become part of a new division Campbell's was establishing, which they intended to call C-Fresh.

C-Fresh was to house all the current and future fresh food aspects of Campbell's program, which at the time consisted of Bolthouse Farms and their fresh soup division.

C-Fresh was going to be run by the current CEO of Bolthouse Farms, Jeff Dunn.

Thus, Jeff was in a precarious position; he had to convince us at Garden Fresh to sell the company to Campbell's. And he had to convince his corporate parent, Campbell's, to cut a check for hundreds of millions of dollars to buy us.

It's not easy to be in the middle of potentially competing interests like that. We at Garden Fresh would naturally like as much money as possible for our company, and Bolthouse's corporate parent, Campbell's Soup, naturally wanted to pay as little as possible for Garden Fresh.

It didn't take long to realize that, while Campbell's was interested in Garden Fresh, their level of interest did not match that of the Bolthouse group.

Ray made it very clear in our first meeting together that "this will not be an Annie's Naturals valuation. We were involved in the bidding for that company and dropped out about two-thirds of the way through. Don't expect that from us for Garden Fresh."

There was tension on our side of the table, too.

Our financial advisors kept asking me why I was so willing to talk to one party and one party only: Campbell's Soup.

This was particularly poignant in light of what General Mills had just paid for Annie's Naturals.

After Ray was so emphatic that Campbell's would not pay for Garden Fresh what General Mills paid for Annie's, the consensus among our advisors was: "If Campbell's won't pay the price that Annie's just went for, why don't you at least go talk to the company that just did pay that price for Annie's? At least approach General Mills."

Furthermore, our accounting firm's investment banking division strongly encouraged us to hire them, put together a book detailing the Garden Fresh opportunity, and market it to potential buyers nationwide.

In other words, conduct an auction for Garden Fresh, ideally start a bidding war, and maximize the partners' value.

They were all great points. But they failed to take into account was all that encompassed this particular partnership's concept of "value."

Knowing Jack and Annette the way I did, after having built this company alongside them for 12 years, I knew that "value" meant a lot more than merely money.

The last thing Jack would ever want to do was to see a marketing book assembled on Garden Fresh and have our numbers shopped all over the country. That's not our style. It's just too public. Plus, it would signal we were formally for sale, which was a position we were not ready to put ourselves in.

Rather, we just wanted to have a private conversation with someone. If we were comfortable with them and if we could agree to a price we were happy with, we'd pull the trigger and sell the company.

It was of paramount importance who would end up owning the company should we indeed sell.

Along those lines the Bolthouse division of the Campbell Soup Company was proving to be uniquely qualified.

At this stage of the negotiations, Bolthouse CEO Jeff Dunn was involving one of his top executives, Scott Laporta, who served as Jeff's chief operating officer and chief financial officer.

Together they formed a team that I thought was not only visionary but incredibly entrepreneurial as well, particularly in light of the fact that they were operating under the auspices of a Fortune 500 company environment.

Their values were completely in sync with ours, and the speed with which the operated was remarkable.

In short, I kept telling Jack and Annette: "They're about as much like us as anyone we're ever likely to find."

The final piece of the puzzle that was so important to us all, particularly to Jack and Annette, was that manufacturing remain in Michigan.

Although we never asked the Bolthouse guys to make that commitment, and they never did, we just believed it made all the business sense in the world to keep our production base where it was and not move it to California.

In addition, Scott Laporta, Bolthouse's COO and CFO, not only reiterated my sense that it made little economic sense to move our manufacturing to California, but he also discussed at length his plans to expand capacity at our plants.

When Jack and I would talk about whether or not Scott was being sincere with us, which I believe he was, I said to Jack: "At some point in this process, we're just going to have to trust them."

So when I added all that up—private conversation versus public auction, genuine visionaries and entrepreneurs who shared our values and bias for action, yet still commanding the resources of a Fortune 500 company that I believed we needed moving forward to compete, with at least a virtual commitment to continue to employ our current work force—everything was pointing in one direction.

To go down this road with one company and one company only: Campbell's.

THE LONG AND WINDING ROAD TO A "NUMBER"

Agreeing to continue the dialogue is one thing. Agreeing to an eventual number in terms of a sales price in quite another.

Our financial advisors were screaming at us not to accept anything under $300 million. They were confident they could, with some minor tweaking, get us that amount in a year or so. Since we were certainly not motivated sellers, what was another year?

Jack wasn't really putting much thought into a number that he and Annette would accept either, although one time he did say "$275 million sounds about right."

Some of our administrative personnel were conducting research on their own and kept producing evidence that came in between Jack's $275 million floor and our financial advisors' $300 million plus ceiling.

Scott Laporta, who by now had taken over for Jeff Dunn as Bolthouse Farms' lead on this deal, was asking me for guidance in terms of what number we were looking for.

I appreciated him reaching out to me in this manner, as I knew he was in a difficult situation trying to convince Campbell's all that he and Jeff could do with Garden Fresh, but that they couldn't do anything unless they actually bought us. We had made, however, a conscious decision to not provide any insight as to what might be acceptable to us, to let Campbell's frame the discussion by throwing the first pitch.

All the while Campbell's financial team in Camden was asking for very detailed financial information, so that whatever offer they did make could be based on a certain rationale. Perfectly understandable, but because we were still essentially a private company that did not expect to be discussing a sale, we had virtually nothing prepared for them.

In the midst of all this, one morning I walked into our administrative office building and Annette came rushing up to me: "Jack's in jail! Jack's in jail!"

Jack and Annette have a second home in Tampa, and Jack had decided to run down there for the weekend. He has a full set of clothes at that house, so all he had to do, in terms of packing, was to throw a magazine in a duffle bag.

Unfortunately, Jack had forgotten that this was the same duffle bag he had taken to the shooting range earlier in the week and that his Glock was at the very bottom, lying underneath a sweatshirt.

And wouldn't you know it—the Glock was loaded, too.

So it's not difficult to imagine the scene at Detroit Metropolitan Airport as Jack was going through security. Attempting to board a plane with a loaded gun is not a good thing.

Soon Jack found himself at the local police station, calling his friends at the Ferndale Police Department, who put in a good word for Jack, and he was soon released.

Typical of Jack's character, though, he said the airport security force was just doing their job, that the mistake was his, and that they could not have been more professional in how they handled the matter.

So anyway, in mid-December, two and a half months after my initial meeting with the Bolthouse guys in Santa Monica, Ray Liguori called and said he wanted to fly into Detroit from Camden and personally present an offer to us. Scott Laporta flew in from Southern California to represent Bolthouse Farms.

Ray's presentation was very straightforward in terms of where he saw the market was currently valuing companies such as Garden Fresh, and he told us Campbell's was prepared to pay between $200 and $220 million for our company—the exact amount I told Jack and Annette back in September that, if we could get, they should accept.

The problem, though, was that by now expectations were certainly higher, with many on our team still believing something in the range of $300 million was attainable.

We conveyed that to Ray and told him and Scott that we'd be back to them in a week or so.

The following week, we sent them a letter countering their offer at $290 million.

On the Friday before Christmas, just as I was walking into my office after returning from a trip to New York, my cell phone rang and Ray Liguori's name popped up on my screen.

I answered and Ray said he had Scott on the line as well.

"Well, Dave. I got your counteroffer, and after I picked myself up off the floor I decided to table any further discussions until after the holidays. No sense all of us ruining our Christmas."

So that was that, at least for a while. Frankly, I was relieved and just felt like enjoying my holidays, and during the holidays I was continuously struck by how at peace I was over the entire matter.

As promised, Ray did reach out to us in early January and said he and Scott wanted to come back in to talk to us.

They did just that, and Ray said he was now willing to raise his floor from $200 million to $220 million. And that there still might be some room left on their side after that.

I told Ray we'd be willing to continue to negotiate for a few more weeks, but that if we could not agree to terms by the end of January we were just going to walk away. We had learned from our previous experiences that discussions of this nature were both draining and distracting. In addition, rumors of Campbell's interest in us had already started to leak within our plants, and it was affecting morale.

Ray readily agreed and we scheduled weekly conference calls for the next couple weeks.

We went back and forth, with Ray finally agreeing to come up to $230 million. At that time I told him we were at $250 million.

Late in the afternoon of the last business day in January, Ray said that even though he thought our number was too high, he had been over-ruled by his CEO and CFO and that they were willing to agree to a price of $240 million. All cash.

Jack had spent much of the month of January at his home in Tampa and was not directly involved in the negotiations.

So early that evening I called Jack and told him we had agreed to a price of $240 million for Garden Fresh.

"Wait," he said. "Are you telling me you just got us $200 million more than I thought the company was worth last September when we were driving up to Traverse City?"

"Yes," I replied.

"Well, good job," he told me.

I did not have the heart to tell him, though, that the chances of us actually closing for $240 million were remote, at best, and that the things that happened from here on out could only hurt us in terms of the price Campbell's would actually pay; no matter how many good things happened between that moment and the time we closed, they'd never pay more than $240 million, only less.

I just let him enjoy his weekend in Tampa.

TAKE TIME TO REFLECT

Within a couple weeks, we signed a non-binding letter of intent with the Campbell Soup Company to sell Garden Fresh for $240 million.

To keep the deal under wraps, Campbell's assigned it a secret internal name, "Project Diamond," ostensibly for Jack's love of softball. I always wondered whether it was because they thought they had found a diamond in the rough.

They soon started sending waves of process engineers to our plants to review our operations.

They also had a team of auditors from Ernst & Young's Philadelphia office come in to review our books and financial records for the past two years.

Jack was overseeing the operations reviews, and our financial people were working with Ernst & Young, although I did make two presentations to the audit team they had assembled.

In early March I also flew out to Santa Monica and had a four-hour presentation/meeting with the Bolthouse C-suite team and their staff.

The following week I flew to Philadelphia to do the same with Campbell's CEO Denise Morrison at their headquarters in Camden, New Jersey.

I arrived at their home office a few minutes early and had time to stroll through the lobby. There was a waiting area with tasteful seating; in addition there was a long corridor where the history of this nearly 150-year-old company was documented. Panel after panel detailed the origins of Campbell Soup and all the strategic moves they've made throughout their lifetime.

As I was waiting for Ray to come out to get me, I couldn't help but think about our history.

Of me developing four marinades on my kitchen counter, packaging them under the brand American Connoisseur and making the first 400,000 units by hand in an unheated commercial kitchen that I financed by having my girlfriend sign for a $2,500 credit card loan.

Of me then buying a mustard company and proceeding to break 800,000 eggs over the course of four years in the mornings and marketing my products in the afternoons.

Of Jack taking the bus to his bankrupt restaurant after his car was repossessed and pulling out that five-gallon bucket to make that first batch of Artichoke Garlic Salsa, hoping it would help pay his electric bill.

Of Jack and Annette threatened to be shut down by the Ferndale city manager for making salsa in the back of their unlicensed restaurant, only to quickly befriend him and move to an abandoned former video store and convert that to a manufacturing facility.

Of how empty the new 25,000-square-foot Garden Fresh salsa plant was the first time I walked into it with Jack, just after he had opened it and just after I had introduced myself to him at that food show in New York.

Of all that we had been through to build Garden Fresh: launching our dip line, buying Basha Hummus, doing our Margaritaville deal, buying the El Matador Tortilla Chip Company, developing our HPP expertise, opening up accounts at virtually every major retailer in the nation by being focused on developing strategic partnerships with them instead of simply trying to sell them something.

After all that, here I was in the lobby of a Fortune 500 company about to put on a presentation to their CEO so that they might purchase us—this company that still made their salsa in five-gallon buckets—for almost a quarter billion dollars.

Ray eventually came down to the lobby and ushered me upstairs to Campbell's C-suite.

My first impression was how austere it was. This was not a company that was spending a lot of their shareholders' money on sleek new office furniture. Good for them.

After we set up in Denise's conference room, she came in with her CFO, Anthony Disilvestro. Scott Laporta from Bolthouse Farms was also there.

Denise could not have been warmer or more gracious. She possessed an understated elegance that instantly connected with me.

She shared with me an internal brochure Campbell's had developed that she said was important to her. It stressed the values she thought Campbell's needed to emphasize, with respect to the work environment her company fostered.

What I found touching about it, though, was the gesture itself. She knew she was dealing with a family company and wanted to stress to me that she got it; that she recognized the value of that kind of culture and that, even though Campbell's was a Fortune 500 company, she knew the more they could operate as a family the better.

She emphasized the point when I asked her: "What's the biggest challenge you face as a CEO of a company like this?"

Without hesitating, she answered: "The culture. We've just got to think differently."

She didn't elaborate, and I didn't ask her to. But I understood why she reached out and paid the price she did to buy Bolthouse Farms.

Sure, strategically she knew she had to pivot from the center of the store to the perimeter, and Bolthouse got her to the produce department. Garden Fresh, in turn, would get her to the deli department. That's why I was there.

But I sensed that deep down she knew Campbell's Soup needed to be more like Jeff Dunn and Scott Laporta: more visionary, more dynamic, more nimble, more in tune, more entrepreneurial.

And less ossified.

In other words, she realized that, while the moves she was taking were strategically sound, deep down she was aware that people like Jeff and Scott were the future of food: forward-thinking, both in terms of product development and management style.

That the more Campbell's was like Bolthouse the better it would be moving forward in the brave world that embodied the food revolution.

That she bought Bolthouse as much for the cultural benefits they offered as she did for the business benefits.

And that if the Bolthouse team wanted Garden Fresh as much as they did, there must be something to us.

I proceeded to the podium and for the next hour and a half walked her through the Garden Fresh saga/phenomenon. I spoke from the heart, did not try to "sell" her anything; this was certainly not the time for that and truly would have been beneath the dignity of the moment.

My biggest surprises were how dialed in she was—truly engaged, bordering on the point of fascination—and how much she was learning. I had the sense she had received a high-level briefing but was enjoying the depth of what was being offered to her.

I'm also convinced she saw in Garden Fresh what she saw in Jeff and Scott and Bolthouse Farms: a bold and dynamic and entrepreneurial culture that, while not perfect, embodied the future of food. Making products by hand if necessary so that you never compromise on flavor profile, yet employing space age technology so that you could still scale national—and beyond.

After the presentation, Scott had to discuss some matters with Anthony privately, so I found myself alone outside Denise's office with Ray.

"Jeff and Scott have never said anything that wasn't positively glowing about the support they've received from Denise. They love her," I said.

"She's amazing," Ray replied. "What they can't see, as they're in California, and I do, as I'm here in New Jersey with her, is all that she has to deal with. The investment community, the analysts, all the events. I don't know how she does it. I couldn't."

―――

HEART MATTERS

It was just our luck that for the first time in our history our sales were down in January from the prior year. Part of it was due to timing issues, part of it was due to some promotional anomalies, part of it was due to the market forces that I sensed were beginning to work against us, which were indeed doing just that.

In my heart I knew that for the foreseeable future we were going to be fine. I had numerous major deals that would kick in throughout the year that would put us on the path to the same steady growth rate we had settled into over the course of the past few years.

But Fortune 500 companies really don't want to hear what's in your heart. They just want to focus on the data they're looking at on their financial spreadsheets.

In other words, numbers matter. Big time. Period.

In early May I was in Austin, Texas, just coming out of a meeting with the co-CEO of Whole Foods, Garden Fresh's fifth largest customer, Walter Robb.

Walter Robb is a business hero of mine. Not only has he been at the forefront of the food revolution, building, in concert with his co-CEO John Mackey, Whole Foods into the premier specialty food chain the world has ever seen, but he's as focused on ensuring Whole Foods makes the world a better place every bit as much as he is on Whole Foods' bottom line.

He's a fervent proponent of conscientious capitalism: that companies can do well by doing good, and that they in fact have a responsibility to do so.

I doubt that any community has benefited more from Walter's brand of conscientious capitalism than Detroit.

A few years ago Walter spearheaded the placement of a Whole Foods Market in the midtown area of downtown Detroit, a place where virtually no food was sold, let alone the high-end variety that is the staple of any Whole Foods store.

It was a big bet, one that took both courage and determination, particularly since Whole Foods signed a 20-year lease on the building.

Walter is on record as saying that the day Whole Foods Market opened in Detroit was one of the greatest days in his professional life. Beautiful. And for what it is worth, that Detroit store is exceeding projections in terms of sales.

After our meeting, Walter ushered me down to the Whole Foods corporate headquarters lobby, and I caught a cab to go back to the airport. Soon my phone rang, and it was Ray Ligouri from Campbell's.

Ray told me he was coming to Detroit to meet with us the next day, that he'd be at our Garden Fresh offices at around 11:30, that he was having Scott Laporta fly in from Santa Monica, and that he insisted Jack and Annette be at the meeting.

By this time it was about 4:00 p.m., and I was thinking two things: one, that it's a good thing we were all going to be in town the next day, as this certainly was extremely short notice, and, two, that I was quite sure Ray was not coming into town with good news.

What also struck me as unusual was that the very next business day, Monday, Campbell's CEO Denise Morrison was scheduled to visit Garden Fresh for the first time, and Ray was going to accompany her.

I told Ray that he did not have to fly into Detroit on Friday only to come back with Denise on Monday, that we could simply discuss whatever he needed to over the phone.

Ray insisted on coming in to see us, though, saying that he needed to button down some issues prior to Denise's arrival, as it would be "awkward" to continue discussions along these lines in her presence.

Although he did not specifically say so, I believed that's why he wanted Jack and Annette present at this meeting as well. He wanted answers prior to leaving, prior to him coming out with Denise on Monday. Until then Jack and Annette had not been directly involved in our negotiations.

My instincts turned out to be right.

Ray told us that, due to Garden Fresh's first-quarter sales struggles, his lack of confidence in the deals we were professing to have coming on line later in the year, and concerns their auditors had found in our overall profit potential, he was lowering Campbell's offer from $240 million to $210 million.

Our discussion was civil yet contentious; we fought Ray on virtually every point he made.

Jack and Annette remained silent throughout.

After an hour and a half or so, it was time for us to say something definitive with respect to what price we were willing to accept. I asked Jack if he needed to step out of the conference room so that we could discuss the matter in private.

"No," he said.

Looking at Ray, he continued: "We're not going to decide this today."

Which meant Ray was going to have to come back with Denise on Monday without a final deal.

Jack then added, talking directly to Ray: "I really don't understand, or care, about profit projections or sales multiples. I just know there's a certain magic to Garden Fresh, and that's what you guys are going to have to value."

It wasn't a calculated statement. It was simply Jack speaking from his heart, how he felt after all he had done and all we'd gone through to build this company to what it had become.

But again, Fortune 500 companies don't care what's in your heart.

Part of me could not help but feel for Ray.

How could he, the vice president of mergers and acquisitions for a Fortune 500 company, a man exceedingly intelligent, with a Wall Street background, possibly convey this notion to his superiors?

I could only imagine Ray going before his board and saying: "Sure, I believe we're overpaying for Garden Fresh. but what we all need to realize is that we're buying magic here, my fellow board members."

He'd be laughed out of Camden with a line like that. Numbers matter to these people; magic is for suckers.

But at that moment there was really nothing Ray could say to Jack, or to any of us at that matter. All he could do was go back to Camden without an answer and come back with his CEO the following Monday.

As he was leaving, Annette said to him, in light of how contentious our discussion was: "Don't worry, Ray. We know you have to act like this."

On Sunday evening, the day before Ray and Denise were to come back to Ferndale, I called Jack at home.

"You know," I said to him. "While Friday's meeting was crazy, I still don't see why we could not have done that over the phone, Ray's right; we do owe them a number. How do you and Annette feel?"

Without hesitation, Jack replied: "Let's go with $231 million."

"$231 million?" I replied.

"Yeah, I think that's right."

I said, "That's a fine number, Jack, but it's a curious one. Do you have any rationale for it?"

"No, not really," he said. "It just feels right in my heart."

On Monday morning he walked into my office and asked me what I was going to do.

I told him that what Annette said to Ray before he left on Friday was right: he was just doing his job, strictly focusing on financial parameters and trying to get the best deal he could for Campbell's in terms of price.

But after spending a couple hours with Denise a couple months ago, my sense was that she was a genuine visionary and that she thought more strategically. I thought her legacy would be determined by the extent to which she got Campbell's from the center of the store to the perimeter of the store.

That's why she bought Bolthouse Farms in 2012 — to enter the produce department.

And that's why Campbell's was interested in buying Garden Fresh now — to get to the deli department.

I told Jack: "I don't think she really cares about the $21 million difference between our camps right now. For the CEO of an $8 billion company, $21 million is a rounding error."

I said: "We are only going to sell this company once, so I'm just going to tell them that $231 million is what's in your heart and that that's the price we'd accept for Garden Fresh."

"Sounds good to me," he said.

As he was leaving my office, he turned around and said one last thing: "High stakes poker, isn't it?"

Denise and Ray flew into Detroit on Campbell's corporate jet, and poor Scott had to fly back in from southern California, even though he was just in Detroit on the previous Friday.

Prior to them all coming to Garden Fresh, they visited a couple local supermarkets.

When I met Denise at our offices, I asked her how her visits went and she said: "I can't believe how much fresh food you guys have out here!"

We all had lunch in our conference room; then Jack took Denise out for a plant tour.

Ray looked at me and said, "Well, Dave, I think you owe me a number."

I told Ray we had a number for him, but that it was a curious one: $231 million. I told him I wished I had a rational explanation for it but that it was simply what was in Jack's heart.

I made it clear that this did not mean that we're now at $231 million and Campbell's is at $210 so maybe we could meet somewhere in the middle. I said $231 million was what we'd accept for the company.

Ray's hand was flat on our conference table and he was looking at it as he tapped it up and down.

"Well," he said. "You've exceeded my authority. I'll have to discuss this with Denise when she gets back."

Blessedly, Jack brought her back a couple minutes later, and Ray asked us for some time alone with her.

Within minutes, Denise herself came out and told us all we had a deal, at Jack's heartfelt $231 million.

Ray later told us that, after visiting the second of the two supermarkets that morning, while they were still in the parking lot and were about to make their way over to Garden Fresh, Denise told him he could go as high as $230 million for us.

And here's Jack coming in at $231 million, just because that's what was in his heart!

To which I could only tell Jack, as we were leaving the office that day: "I sure wish your heart had told you $233 million."

Secret 7: Walk the Talk and Everything Comes Together

We had entered the dark room. Many of them, in fact. We had found our place in this world, and we did whatever we had to do to maintain that position. We searched for and eventually found several Holy Grails. We committed ourselves to the antithesis of conventional sales techniques and instead strove to form genuine partnerships with our customers. We didn't just develop products: we developed strategic advantages our competitors could not match.

All this resulted in a company that exceeded even our wildest initial expectations. Even our wildest dreams.

Continued

Continued

It also resulted in a company that was highly desirable. We were solicited for years by both financial and strategic buyers.

In the end we sold to a purchaser whose values were in alignment with our own, to a greater extent than anyone else we were in discussions with.

That mattered more to us than sheer price optimization. We never did conduct a national auction, as many were advising us to do.

We sold Garden Fresh for almost a quarter of a billion dollars. That's an enormous sum of money.

We're at peace with the people we sold Garden Fresh to—to a greater extent than if we had sold it to someone who would not have maintained what we had built. Even if we could have gotten twice that amount.

That peace is worth more than money.

EPILOGUE

AFTER DENISE, SCOTT, AND RAY LEFT GARDEN FRESH that day, it took another month and a half to finalize the purchase agreement, which ended up being over 100 pages long, and close our deal.

When the deal finally did close, Jack wasn't even with us. He was on a five-hour layover at JFK waiting to board a flight to Detroit, as he had spent the weekend playing softball in the Dominican Republic.

Not that it mattered, for no one was in a celebratory mood. Instead, a sense of relief ruled the moment.

It had been just over nine months since my first meeting with Jeff Dunn and Scott Laporta in Santa Monica. More than six months since Ray Liguori flew to Detroit to present Campbell's initial offer.

"The longest six months of my life," Jack told me.

"I hated it all," Annette has since said.

I understood how they felt.

One would think selling your company and finally realizing the pot of gold at the end of that entrepreneurial rainbow would be a wonderful experience. In fact, it's the antithesis of that.

We all knew that going in, based on our previous experiences with Nestlé and Pepsi. In a deal of this nature, once you agree to a price you're automatically thrust into a position of defending it.

We defended it as best we could for those long six months that Jack referenced.

It had been a bruising process, and we all needed time to heal.

The feeling in our Garden Fresh C-suite, though, was in stark contrast to the response we were getting from the metro Detroit community.

Once the deal was announced, we were stunned by the reaction. People were thrilled that this local company, with it's humblest of origins, could attract the interest of a Fortune 500 company.

Even the local media, who soon descended on our Garden Fresh campus, were positively giddy in their coverage. They just could not stop smiling as they were filing their reports.

Fox2 News Detroit anchor and reporter Charlie Langton described the moment as well as anyone:

"I knew of Garden Fresh, and when I got word of the Campbell's deal and heard about the incredible amount of money involved, I headed over to your offices.

"This is the part that got me; I like the common guy, that's the angle I take. And when I showed up, within two minutes I could tell the workers loved their jobs. And they loved you guys. They all felt like millionaires.

"Then I met you guys and I could sense the camaraderie.

"There was just the perfect combination of pride and respect at Garden Fresh. That to me is the true sign of a successful company. That captured the spirit of this deal. You could feel it."

The deal was a national media event as well, covered in *The Wall Street Journal,* on CNBC, in *The New York Times*, and *USA Today*.

But the reaction was not as positive on the national food scene.

Shortly before the deal was formally announced, I was in Atlanta at a food show and ran into Whole Foods co-CEO Walter Robb. He hugged me upon seeing me, as is his custom. I told him what was about to transpire, as it was important to me he hear about it directly from me.

As what I was telling Walter began to sink in, his shoulders sagged and his knees buckled in disappointment. He had a crestfallen look on his face.

For here was a company, Garden Fresh, that had exemplified the food revolution in this country. Making genuine, authentic products. Fresh, all natural. That had maintained their principles, even to the point of making their salsa by hand in five-gallon buckets just to ensure that the product they were putting out on the market was the very best it could be.

Now all that would be at risk in the hands of what had come to be known as "Big Food." That a Fortune 500 company could never maintain the spirit that built Garden Fresh. That something would surely be lost in the translation.

Walter didn't say any of that to me, but he didn't have to; the look on his face, his body language, said it all.

And soon, as our other accounts found out about the deal, those sentiments were expressed directly to me.

I certainly understood how Walter and others felt.

But what they could not possibly know were the particulars of this situation that, in my heart, made this deal so right.

I still believed the current Garden Fresh management group had taken the company as far as we could and that market forces were starting to work against us and, unless we associated ourselves with the resources of a significantly larger entity, we stood a good chance of being overwhelmed on our retailers' shelves.

Soon Garden Fresh might start to shrink instead of to grow.

But even in the face of all that, I still would have been willing to continue the fight, and I would not have bet against us in terms of continuing to make Garden Fresh something great, had I not believed so much in who would end up with Garden Fresh.

In the nine months since I had met Bolthouse CEO Jeff Dunn, nothing dissuaded me from my initial impression garnered during our first meeting in his offices in Santa Monica: this guy "gets it." He's an entrepreneur at heart who is passionate about changing the way people eat and who believes that doing so requires food manufacturers to change.

Dunn loves our five-gallon buckets.

Similarly, Scott Laporta, who was soon to be named president of Bolthouse Farms, had earned both my respect and admiration.

We crossed paths with a lot of very intelligent people over the course of putting this deal together. People don't make it to the upper echelons of Fortune 500 companies without being smart. Without being talented. Without being driven.

Scott possessed all those qualities. What set him apart, though, is while you certainly need a high IQ to perform at this level. If you don't have at least one person on the other side of the table with a high EQ your deal is in trouble.

For Campbell's that someone was Scott Laporta: very high IQ, equally high EQ. There were many moments when we not only needed Scott's intelligence, but we needed a voice of reason as well.

Scott was the person Nestlé and Osem and Frito-Lay and Strauss did not have. Our deal with Campbell's would not have closed without him.

If there is anything I wish I had said to Campbell's CEO Denise Morrison on that fateful day when we finally agreed to Jack's heartfelt number of $231 million, it's that I hope she realizes how fortunate she is to be associated with executives like Jeff and Scott.

Together they had identified a strategic target in Garden Fresh. Reached out to it unsolicited. Made us comfortable enough to not only abandon a multi-year exit strategy but to enter into exclusive negotiations with them. Agreed to terms with us, then persuaded the Campbell's board to approve it all.

What they accomplished was not only textbook, but masterful.

I also believed Denise Morrison would continue to support them at the level she was already demonstrating at Bolthouse Farms.

It was not lost on me that, while so many of the center-of-the-store-oriented Fortune 500 food companies were responding to the fresh food revolution by merely cutting costs, she was guiding her company to the areas in the supermarket where growth was occurring, to the perimeter of the store, to produce and deli, even though margins were traditionally smaller there.

Thus, she was taking the current cash flow from her company's historic lines, which were ceasing to grow, and plowing those profits into categories her company had never played in before.

In short, she was every bit the visionary that Jeff and Scott were. She "got it" too.

They had earned my confidence. I just didn't believe there was any way they were going to destroy any of the value that we had poured our hearts and souls into creating.

These were the right people to entrust with Garden Fresh.

So we did just that.

One of the first things Jack and Annette did, after the funds were distributed, was set up a charitable foundation, which is how they'd like to spend the rest of their time, helping those in the metro Detroit community less fortunate than themselves.

They're naming it the "Artichoke Garlic Foundation," in honor of that first variety of fresh salsa Jack made in the back of their bankrupt restaurant just outside of Detroit.

YOU NEVER KNOW WHICH SWITCH WILL ILLUMINATE YOUR DARK ROOM

I told Campbell's I was willing to stay on for six months as a consultant, but that was it. They deserved to run the company as they saw fit, without any of the "old guard" standing in their way.

So this chapter of my entrepreneurial life was coming to an end.

But I've always been struck by how close it came to never even starting.

A couple days after I met Jack for the first time at that food show in New York, I sent him a detailed two-page e-mail, laying out my vision to produce my salad dressings made with whole cloves of garlic under his Garden Fresh Gourmet label.

After a few weeks, I had not heard back from him. I told my wife I thought that was strange, as it had seemed Jack was genuinely intrigued by the idea. Plus, I felt a certain special connection to him.

Of course, now I know that due to Jack's extraordinary charisma everyone feels a special connection to him. But at the time I had no idea that was the case.

So I decided to call Jack. He answered the phone, said he remembered me, said he loved my idea, and invited me to lunch the very next day in Ferndale.

At that lunch he told me he feared he had overbuilt his new salsa plant. That maybe everyone who told him you don't go from a 3,000-square-foot facility to a 25,000-square-foot facility, that you don't increase your size eightfold, was right.

That it might be a good idea for me to move my Mucky Duck Mustard Company production into his huge new plant and outsource the manufacturing to Garden Fresh. He said that would help him pay his rent.

I did just that, and you've just read all that's happened since.

I consider that phone call to Jack, following up on the e-mail he never responded to, as the defining moment of my professional life, the floodlight that fully, finally, lit the dark room I had been in for so long. It signaled the beginning of the end of my lost decade.

Had I never made that follow-up call, had I just assumed Jack did not think me making salad dressings under his Garden Fresh label was such a good idea after all, our partnership, our adventures together, would never have happened.

No number 1 brand of fresh salsa in the United States. No premiere deli supply company in the country. None of our charitable efforts. No 450+ employees. No $110 million in revenue.

And no sale to a Fortune 500 company for almost a quarter of a billion dollars.

And chances are good that neither of Jack nor I would be living the life we imagined for ourselves.

A couple months after Jack and I became partners, I was curious: "Hey, Jack, I'm wondering. Do you remember that e-mail I sent you, after the Fancy Food Show in New York?"

"What e-mail?" he asked.

"The one where I laid out that plan for me to make my salad dressings under your label. You never responded to it."

"Where did you send it?" he asked.

"To the address on your business card."

"Oh," he said. "My daughter made up our cards and put that address on there. "

"So what?" I asked.

Jack breezily, nonchalantly responded:

"I don't do e-mail."

INDEX

Artichoke Garlic Foundation, 159
Authenticity: Costco buyer on Garden
Fresh Salsa's, 32–34; of the Garden
Fresh Gourmet Salsa ingredients,
28–29; of the Garden Fresh Salsa
manufacturing process, 29–31
Avure, 85, 88

B

Basha Foods: forgiveness following
dispute between Garden Fresh and,
99–103; Garden Fresh purchase
of, 81–84, 102–103, 105, 118, 145;
as leading brand of hummus in
the metro Detroit market, 82, 99;
preservatives added to the "all
natural line" of hummus of, 84;
proficiency in DSD (direct store
delivery) by, 100–101
"Big Food," 157
"Black Swans" taverns (England), 38
Bolthouse Farms: HPP technology used
by, 130; Jeff Dunn reaching out to
Dave on behalf of, 127, 128; purchased
by Campbell Soup Company, 126, 127,
129, 134, 145–146, 151, 159; similarities
of Garden Fresh and, 130–131;
tension over Garden Fresh purchase
between Campbell and, 137–139
Bottled water products, 46
Boys and Girls Club (Detroit), 117
Brand standard: authenticity as part
of the Garden Fresh Salsa, 28–31;
creating more value by making less
money and a high, 34–35; deciding to
find our place by developing a, 19–21;
designing a unique label for Garden
Fresh Salsa matching their, 25–28;
Garden Fresh's promise to be the
best as their, 20–21, 31–32; how the
Costco buyer validated their, 31–34.
See also Products
Buddies Foods, 96–99, 118
Buffett, Jimmy, 72, 117
Building a company. *See* Strategic
development
Buyers: being open-minded about the
needs of your, 53; Garden Fresh's

PowerPoint presentation to, 59–62;
melt away the skepticism of, 63–65;
remembering that they need to see
your C-suite, 56–58; what not to
bring when you see, 53–56. *See also*
Strategic partnerships

C

C-suite: making it visible to your buyers,
56–58; true strategic partnerships
formed by the, 58
Campbell Soup Company: agreeing
on a purchase price and terms for
Garden Fresh, 140–152; Bolthouse
Farms purchased by, 126, 127, 129, 134,
145–146, 151, 159; Denise Morrison
on core values of, 145; process of
purchasing Garden Fresh Gourmet,
132–152; tension over Garden Fresh
purchase between Bolthouse and,
137–139; their plans to have Garden
Fresh become C-Fresh division, 137.
See also Morrison, Denise
Children's Hospital (Detroit), 116
Chuck and Dave, 96–99, 118
Churchill, Winston, 1
Clubhouse Bar-B-Q, 7–8, 61, 70
CNBC, 156
Coca-Cola Company, 105, 134
Compassion core value, 116–118
Competitive advantage: building a
company with, 94; Garden Fresh's
strategy path to building a, 69–93; just
showing up as being half the battle
to, 93
Core values: compassion, 116–118;
Denise Morrison on Campbell's,
145; do you value values?, 120–121;
forgiveness, 99–103; importance
of not compromising your, 95–96;
resolve, 96–99; respect and dignity,
51–56, 104–115, 156; the value of
having, 118–120
Costco: attempting to get Garden
Fresh products into, 21–22; Garden
Fresh brand standard validated by
the buyer from, 31–34; as one of the
largest sellers of food, 21; solving the

H